Community :

How to start a com
and keep it going

Caroline Pinder

National Extension College/National Federation of Community Organisations

The Author

Caroline Pinder, aged 34, has an Open University degree and an HND in Business Studies. After spending many years as a volunteer setting up a variety of community projects, Caroline was employed as Organising Secretary of one of the country's largest Councils for Voluntary Service. She also spent 18 months working as a Community Consultant, and is currently employed at the St. Helens Information Technology Centre where she is responsible for the Centre's Open Access programme for local small businesses and community groups.

Caroline has been a local councillor and a school governor; she has a thirteen year old daughter, and is a Justice of the Peace in Cheshire where she now lives.

Acknowledgements

Many people and organisations have contributed to **Community Start Up** and we would like to thank them all. However, special thanks should go to Shell U.K. Ltd., The Esmee Fairbairn Charitable Trust and The Hilden Charitable Fund for their financial support for the project. It would not have been possible without them.

We would also like to thank Margaret Catterill of Earlstown Opportunity Group, Dave Howell of the Feltham Community Association, Pam Ward of Macclesfield Women's Aid and Claudette Griffiths of the Sickle Cell Society for the case studies used in the book. Thanks should also go to Hazel Barbour of Shell U.K. for her enthusiasm and support, Bevan Jones of the National Federation of Community Organisations and Ros Morpeth of the National Extension College, Brendan Flynn, Jo Jenkins, John Kiddle, Katie Taylor, Voluntary Action magazine and to Sue Miles who performed miracles. The illustrations in Chapter 6 are reproduced by kind permission of the Hackney Community Accountancy Project.

Edited by Bevan Jones
Design Mick Keates 01-381 6853
Cartoons Sam Smith 01-286 9361
Typesetting Concise Graphics 01-381 4230
Print NEC Print (National Extension College Trust Ltd,
18 Brooklands Avenue, Cambridge CB2 2HN)
Published by the National Extension College
and the National Federation of Community Organisations
© 1985 all rights reserved
ISBN 0 86082 572 8

GLOSSARY

Like all professions community work is littered with abbreviations which can be very confusing to the newcomer. This is a quick glossary of those most commonly used:

C A – Community Association

C A B – Citizens Advice Bureau

C D A – Co-operative Development Agency

C H C – Community Health Council

C P – Community Programme

C S V – Community Service Volunteers

C V S – Council for Voluntary Service

D E S – Department of Education and Science

D H S S – Department of Health & Social Security

D o E – Department of Employment; also Department of Environment

I Te C – Information Technology Centre

M S C – Manpower Services Commission

N C V O – National Council for Voluntary Organisations

N F C O – National Federation of Community Organisations

R C C – Rural Community Council

V S U – Voluntary Services Unit (at the Home Office)

Y O P – Youth Opportunities Programme, replaced by YTS

Y T S – Youth Training Scheme

CONTENTS

1 SUCCESS STORIES

▷ The Sickle Cell Society
▷ Feltham Community Association
▷ Macclesfield Womens' Aid
▷ The St. Helens & District
   Handicapped Children's Trust and
   the Earlstown Opportunity Group
▷ Sunnyside Community Gardens

▷The Sickle Cell Society

In March 1977 a representative from a recently formed voluntary group OSCAR (Organisation for Sickle Cell Anaemia Research) was invited to a study day on sickle cell disease at London's Central Middlesex Hospital. The idea of starting a local self-help group came up and a few weeks later a group of patients, parents, health workers and others living and working in the London Borough of Brent set up the first branch of OSCAR. They decided to meet monthly and chose as their main objectives improving public awareness about the disease, supporting affected families and raising funds.

Sickle cell disease is the medical name for a group of disorders of the blood. It is an inherited illness found in people whose families come from those parts of the world where there is malaria. It affects those of Afro-Caribbean origin, but also people of mediterranean, Asian and Arab origin. There is no cure for the disease, although the painful symptoms can be alleviated with proper care. Parents can be tested to see whether their blood carries traits of the disease which may be passed on to their children.

In 1977, few people, including the medical profession, were fully aware of the disease and its effects on sufferers and their families. This meant sufferers had no one to talk to about their illness; nor could they and their families get together to talk about the problems it caused them. So, a major challenge facing the newly formed group was to educate the health profession, as well as teachers, social workers and others who came into contact with sufferers. The OSCAR group members also wanted to reach individual patients so they could meet together and feel less isolated.

During the next two years the first leaflet on sickle cell disease was printed, over £1,000 was raised and a series of talks and social outings were organised. The group received considerable support from both the Harlesden Community Project and Brent Community Health Council which helped with postage and subsequently became the base for the monthly meetings.

Contact was made with the black media such as West Indian World Newspaper and Alex Pascall's 'Black Londoners' radio programme as well as with other local newspapers. Due to the novelty of such a self-help group, it received useful publicity. Articles also appeared in medical journals.

In 1979, Brent OSCAR decided to go independent because its members had different objectives to the parent body. It became the Sickle Cell Society, with the aim of becoming a national self-help group with branches around the country. It also wanted to campaign for better services for people with the disease and for more research into treatment and prevention.

Over the next few years the Society continued to develop good links with the media. It persuaded the Health Education Council to produce a series of leaflets for teachers, G.P.s, nurses and other health workers.

Until 1983 the Society was run by its members, with voluntary support from professional health workers. They arranged social functions and outings for members, distributed a newsletter and formed small local groups across the country. Then, in 1983, grants from the Department of Health & Social Security and the Greater London Council enabled them to appoint a full-time secretary. The worker's job was to deal with the increasing amount of correspondence and to extend the Society's publicity campaign.

As a result the Society has been able to increase its publications, give more talks to other community groups, raise more funds to help families affected by the disease, and achieve a four-fold increase in membership.

Now, the Society's priorities are to increase their welfare fund, and to launch a campaign which will involve distributing posters around the country's health centres, clinics and hospitals.

▶Feltham Community Association

"In the early years we made the mistake of underestimating the strength of the organisation and the role it had to play in the community" says the Secretary of Feltham Community Association. "Now we are trying to be more outward-looking and professional in our dealings with the local authority. We are trying to move towards a community partnership with them."

Feltham Community Association was started ten years ago by local voluntary organisations and trade unionists. They believed that the rapid expansion of the area which occurred with the development of Heathrow airport had damaged the local community's identity. There were no social or welfare facilities in the area and the local council gave no encouragement to fill this void.

The first stage was to call a public meeting of all the people who were likely to be interested in starting a community association. This included representatives from all political parties, churches, health and social welfare staff, and individuals living in the area. The meeting led to the formation of the Association whose principal aim at that stage was to obtain premises for a social and community centre.

For the first two years they had no building but still managed to run a full programme of activities with special events for the young and elderly.

After two years of extensive lobbying, which included presenting a petition and organising a motorcade, the local council agreed to give them a redundant, semi-derelict school. Members hastily repaired and re-decorated it.

Over the years FCA has become an 'umbrella' organisation for most of the other voluntary groups in the town, many of which were initiated by the Association. In addition, they have set up several smaller neighbourhood centres in the Feltham area as well as directly running a number of community projects, such as a local resources centre which provides other community groups with facilities like printing, volunteer training and equipment hire.

Good links with the Musicians Union have helped the Centre provide a wide variety of live entertainment attracting large numbers of local residents. FCA has some 1500 members and many more supporters who visit the Centre for the regular social and sporting events. In addition, over 50 local voluntary groups are affiliated to the Association and are able to use the Centre's facilities and services.

Apart from use of the building for a low rent, the Association has had no financial support from the local council other than a grant to build a toilet block. Nor have they had grants from any other tiers of government partly because Feltham is not a priority area for government support, but also because members have wanted to preserve FCA's independence from all political parties.

This has meant that income from the licensed bar is critical for FCA's survival, but at the same time the Association has been anxious not to fall into the trap commonly experienced by community associations of allowing the bar to become the focal point of their work. For this reason, and also to get around the restrictions of charity law, a separate organisation was set up to run the bar, which then donated its profits back to the Association. Its members are now able to concentrate their efforts on promoting local voluntary activity.

Most of the work of running the Centre is done voluntarily by members and reflects their personal involvement. For example, local artist, Peter Howson, has painted magnificent murals around the walls of the main hall telling the story of the Centre and its users. Several years ago, however, because of the growing use of the Centre, it was decided to employ two people to share all the routine administrative and cleaning tasks. These employees are paid out of the Association's income from the bar and their fund-raising events.

Because of the triple need to raise income for the Association, create new employment opportunities for members, and to maintain an adequate level of support for other local voluntary groups, the Association has now set up the Resources Centre. This is a separate organisation which donates its profits back to FCA It is run as a neighbourhood co-operative providing a range of small-scale services such as minor building and repair work, a local courier service, printing, cleaning, which combined make a viable business, as well as serving the needs of voluntary groups, local entrepreneurs, and local residents generally.

In 1987 the building is due to be demolished by the local council to make way for a new office development. If the Association is unable to persuade the council to change its mind, it hopes to be able to raise the funds to buy the Centre. To do this they will have to approach charitable trusts, local industry, the community and government grant-making agencies. They believe the way to do this is to adopt a far more professional and business-like approach to fund-raising and publicity.

"We have to change the old image that 'community' means 'amateur'" says their Secretary. "We have had to stop and think about our public image and this has made us realise that the part played by FCA in the community is as vital as the part played by local business and the various government agencies."

▷ Macclesfield Womens' Aid

The Macclesfield Womens' Aid group began in the summer of 1976 when a county councillor read a story in the local paper about some children and mothers from the Manchester Womens' Refuge who were on a camping holiday at a farm near Macclesfield. He called a meeting at his home of friends and other local people he thought would be interested in helping start a refuge for Macclesfield women. These original members included social workers, the town's NSPCC officer, and local feminists.

"Defining objectives seemed easy" says the current Secretary of the group who has been a member since 1976. "We thought all we had to do was find a property and everything else would follow from that."

Unfortunately, it turned out not to be so easy. "We chased one property after another, paying little attention to whether or not they were really suitable, or how we were going to run a Refuge if ever we succeeded in opening one" continues the Secretary. "Looking back, I think our ideas at that time were too radical for a small town, and, naively, we were surprised that the local council would not co-operate, but seemed to go out of their way to thwart us."

Eventually, in 1978, the group obtained a short-life lease on a house which was under threat of demolition for construction of a new road. But within a few weeks the house proved too small and the group found the running of the Refuge took more time than they realised. A woman living close by volunteered to do some of the day-to-day work at the Refuge. But, after a while, she began to find it was more demanding than a full-time job and it was impractical for her to be on call day and night.

It was at this stage that differences between members of the group emerged. Some felt they should have organised themselves better by going for greater financial security and public recognition for the project before opening the Refuge, whilst others felt the existing situation could be resolved.

The Refuge remained open for three years but as committee members left and moved out of town, the pressures on remaining members with full-time jobs became too great. The project was closed down when a ceiling collapsed in a back bedroom.

"We don't regret the way things turned out" says the

Secretary. "We learnt a lot from those early days, and the second time round we were absolutely clear about what we wanted and the best way to get it."

The passage of time also helped as new legislation was introduced bringing greater national publicity about the problems facing battered women.

Ironically, the group's revival was actively encouraged by the Borough Council whose housing officers had by now become responsible for accommodating battered women under the new Homeless Persons Act. Co-operation also came from other government departments whose staff were feeling the impact of the lack of provision for battered women in the town.

The initiative for reviving the group came from the local Labour Party's Womens' Section, some of whom had been involved with the earlier Refuge. They contacted other original members and together thrashed out a list of aims for the new group and allocated tasks to each member. Problem areas were discussed in great detail, and a policy and philosophy were established for the project.

They now decided two criteria had to be met before a Refuge could function properly. Firstly there had to be assistance from the local council in obtaining a suitable house; secondly they had to have the funds to enable them to employ at least one person to run it.

Once a detailed plan had been established, both problems were overcome relatively easily. The Borough Council offered them a larger house which, although not perfect, was more suitable than the previous property. The Manpower Services Commission agreed to pay the salaries of one full-time and three part-time staff under the Community Programme, a government-funded temporary employment scheme. Once staff were employed, detailed consideration had to be given to the group's responsibilities as an employer and they had to study such things as legislation relating to contracts of employment.

Macclesfield Refuge opened for the second time in 1983 and the group are pleased at the way it is now working. Although the house is again on a short-let, the Council has indicated that a better property will become available. Staff and volunteer members are able to spend more time making contacts with local teachers and other community groups about the problems facing battered women and their children. They are now hoping to open a Womens' Advice Centre in the town as an extension to the Refuge, and to start an aftercare support group.

▷ The St. Helens & District Handicapped Children's Trust and the Earlstown Opportunity Group

In 1981 health and social service workers in St. Helens met together to discuss how local services for handicapped children and their parents could be co-ordinated and improved. With the help of a student and a social work trainee they arranged for a study to be made of how many handicapped children there were in the town and what use they made of the services which were available to them.

The results of that research showed that many parents were either unaware or confused about the services on offer. So, it was decided to call together parents and professional workers to look at how this situation could be changed.

The result of that day-long meeting was the setting up of the St. Helens & District Handicapped Children's Trust. Its aims were to collect and distribute information about local services for handicapped children and to provide the means for them and their parents to meet together to exchange information and break down their social isolation.

They achieved the first of these aims by producing a booklet which was distributed to all families in the area with a handicapped child. It was also given to the parents of newly-born handicapped children by the local paediatrician, who became the link person between the family and other health and social service staff.

The Trust's second initiative was to establish an Opportunity Group for children under 5 years and their parents. Opportunity Groups exist in many towns in the U.K.: they are simply playgroups for handicapped children which the parents run. Non-handicapped and older children of the families are also encouraged to come along during school holidays so there is complete integration of handicapped and non-handicapped.

The Trust's Opportunity Group first opened in 1981 for two mornings a week with ten children, using a small church hall. These premises soon proved unsuitable on two counts: firstly, all the equipment had to be removed from the building after each session. Secondly, there were requests from social workers to take children from the 'at risk' register. They were handicapped in ways not previously defined by the Trust's members and it became clear that the group required larger, more permanent premises. So it moved to another church hall in a different part of the town.

Now the group has 29 children on its register. It runs three sessions a week, one of which is restricted to severely handicapped children so they can be given special attention and encouraged to make full use of their limited abilities.

Since the start of the group the involvement of parents has been seen as essential by the Trust's members. Although few parents have chosen to get involved in the Trust in any formal way, they do participate fully in the day-to-day running of the playgroup and its fund-raising activities. Additional volunteers have been recruited to work at the playgroup; they are also encouraged to bring their own children along.

Since 1981 the group has been receiving an annual grant under the Urban Aid scheme. This grant is for five years and covers the expenses of a co-ordinator and two assistants, rent, overheads, and petrol for the minibus they borrow from another local voluntary group to transport parents and children to and from the playgroup.

The urban aid grant for the group will run out in two years' time and they are exploring other means of funding. They want to retain their voluntary status which they see as a very important feature of the group. Parents feel that the Opportunity Group acts as a bridge between them and the Social Services department, and the support they receive from the staff and other parents there helps them to come to terms with their child's handicap.

They are now in the process of setting up a scheme to convert a disused school into a children's and community centre.

▷Sunnyside Community Gardens

Sunnyside Community Gardens Project began in 1977 when local Tenants' Associations, community groups and schools got together under the auspices of the North Islington Housing Rights Project to do something about one of the local eyesores – an area of demolished housing which for years past had been surrounded by dilapidated corrugated iron. The new group managed to lease the site from the Greater London Council –

the land is now owned by Islington — clear it of rubble, and, with the help of Community Service Volunteers, landscape it and plant it out as a public open space. The difference with this open space, however, was that it would be managed and maintained entirely by local residents, the Sunnyside Gardeners' Group, and serve as a community resource in an area of high-density housing and few private gardens.

Sunnyside was opened with a grand festival in 1978 and operated for some years with a high level of local involvement, regular school and club projects, weekly work sessions and an annual neighbourhood festival. In 1980 the Inner London Education Authority, via the Islington Adult Education Institute, agreed to fund a co-ordinator to the Project to oversee administration and the development of activities in the Gardens. This post amounts to only 200 hours per year and highlights one of the problems at Sunnyside: no **regular** source of grant-aid, especially for revenue expenditure, and totally inadequate funding of worker hours. Consequently, it proved very hard to maintain continuity in the Gardens and to sustain the very high level of local involvement. By 1982 the project was broke and membership minimal. It was in response to this situation that the Sunnyside Community Gardens Project launched a major redevelopment of the Gardens. This involved an improvements programme which would give rise to a whole new range of activities — all of them with the aim of giving local people not just access to open space but the chance of work with, and have closer contact with, growing things, both wild and cultivated; and through this to a whole range of experiences normally denied to residents of the inner city. Beyond this, it is intended to use the Gardens as the focus of a movement which will spread beyond the immediate site, helping with the planning and planting of communal areas on estates, school nature plots, neglected gardens, window boxes, balconies — even with advice on indoor plants — so having an impact on the appearance of the neighbourhood as a whole.

The first priority was that of **obtaining funding** — a very time-consuming process in itself. Sunnyside has now raised money for capital expenditure from the following sources: Brighter Islington Campaign, the GLC, Urban Aid, Shell Better Britain Campaign, the Allen Lane/British Trust for Conservation Volunteers Tree Planting Campaign. For revenue expenditure the project has continued to depend on its own fund-raising activities.

It would have been impossible to make progress at Sunnyside without the support of **more paid workers.** There are now two part-time workers in addition to the co-ordinator. One is funded through the GLC, the other seconded from the British Trust for Conservation Volunteers. The contracts for both workers expired in October 1984 however, and maintaining worker support and adequate funding for Sunnyside will of necessity remain a major preoccupation.

To accommodate the expanded staff and additional activities, the group had to look for **new office space.** It has therefore moved from the Community Flat on Hornsey Lane Estate to a larger room within the Crouch Hill Recreation Centre.

The remaining members of the Gardens Project took part in a planning exercise to design themselves the new features which were to be constructed on the site. From this came the first phase of their **'Improvements Programme'**. Again with the help of Community Service Volunteers three major tasks are being undertaken in the Gardens. These are: landscaping work and planting a new environmental or **'Wild Area'**; terracing of the north end of the site to provide 14 individual **'Project Plots'** for allocation to schools, groups and individuals; and the construction of a **garden for the elderly and disabled** residents.

The most ambitious fund-raising event in 1983 was the **'Walk on the Wild Side'** – a sponsored 10-mile walk beginning and ending at Sunnyside linking all the open spaces, parks and wildlife sites in Islington. 42 people took part and between them raised over £250 for Sunnyside Gardens and Freightliners City Farm.

Instead of running its own festival in 1983, the project put together **a stall** which it toured to other neighbourhood festivals and similar events throughout the Borough.

2 INTRODUCTION

▷ Types of community groups
▷ How to use this book

▷ Types of community groups

The five stories featured at the beginning of this book are typical of the way people are getting together around and across the country to improve the standard and quality of their own lives. Every day the newspapers contain similar stories.

Community groups are started in a variety of ways:

● **spontaneously** – for example, when a child is knocked down by a car on a busy road through a housing estate, the neighbours decide to petition their local council to provide a zebra crossing.

● **through individuals wanting to make contact with others in a similar predicament,** so they can share their experiences, in much the same way that the Sickle Cell Society was born.

● **with the aid of community workers,** usually employed by the local council, whose job is to bring people together and encourage them to participate in the development of their neighbourhood.

However they start, they are all called community groups because their members have a common interest. They are also voluntary organisations because their activities are outside the framework of the welfare state.

There are many types of community group varying in their aims and the way they are run. Most groups contain elements of several types. Here are some of the main kinds of group:

● **self-help groups:** these exist to help their own members. All of our five examples fall into this category.

● **minority interest groups:** these try to improve the lives of minority groups in the population. The Sickle Cell Society, Macclesfield Women's Aid group, and the Earlstown Opportunity Playgroup can all be described in this way.

● **action, or pressure, groups:** these seek to influence the decision-makers in the interests of the whole community. Feltham Community Association could be defined as an action group. It also tries to represent the community's views and liaise with other agencies on behalf of the community.

● **welfare groups:** these provide a specific service to other people. The involvement of professional staff in the Macclesfield Women's Aid group and the St. Helens & District Handicapped Children's Trust can both be described in this way. The Earlstown Opportunity Playgroup is just one of the services which the latter provides for others.

● **social groups:** members of these are primarily concerned with organising social events. But, again, for all of our five examples the social element is a very important part of their work.

And community groups can change in character over time. For example, the friendships made during the campaign to persuade the local council to put a zebra crossing over a dangerous road may lead to the formation of a permanent tenants' or residents' association which will go on to seek other improvements in the neighbourhood.

It is this capacity for flexibility which has made the voluntary and community sector the pioneering force behind many of the services now provided by the welfare state. Almost ten years after the first Women's Aid Refuge was opened, the Homeless Persons Act was passed giving local authorities a duty to meet the special needs of victims of domestic violence. Health authorities are now recognising the value of setting up centres at local hospitals for people with sickle cell disease. And so on.

Community action achieves change by a bottom-to-top approach, as opposed to imposing legislation on people who have had virtually no say in its making. Community politics have become an integral part of our political system and all the major parties profess to give it their full support.

But the complexity of the state bureaucracy often makes it difficult for community groups to get their views heard. Often, the paperwork and the need to comply with a host of legalities demand time and expertise which is not always available to volunteers. In these circumstances it is easy for community groups to be put off from their struggle because the paperwork assumes a greater importance than the members' real aims.

The purpose of this book is to lay the groundwork for dealing with these administrative tasks so that more of your time and energy can be put to participating in the development of your community.

▷How to use this book

● **on your own** – if you have recently become involved in a community group, or are considering doing so, you can either read quickly through the whole book and then use it as a reference book, or just choose those chapters which deal with the particular task you will be taking on, such as Chapter 6 for Treasurers; Chapter 8 for Publicity Officers, etc.

● **with friends or other members of the group** – if you and some friends are considering starting a community group, or if the group is already established, you can either work your way through the book together, or read a few chapters each and then exchange ideas.

● **as a reference book** – either on your own or with other members of the group. You may prefer only to read sections of the book as and when you need to. The Contents List will help you select relevant sections.

If you have any difficulty using this book or if it doesn't answer your particular question, look at Chapter 12 for lists of other books which go into more detail about specific aspects, and also the list of voluntary organisations which can give you further advice and assistance. Or you can contact a community worker at your local social services department or Council for Voluntary Service.

3 GETTING STARTED

▷ Starting an action group
▷ Working out your objectives
▷ How to carry out research
▷ Your first public meeting

LIBRARY NOTICE BOARD

SUNNYSIDE GARDENS

THERE WILL BE A MEETING OF THE ABOVE ORGANISATION THE FIRST MONDAY OF EVERY MONTH UPSTAIRS AT THE 'SWAN' PUBLIC HOUSE, 16 HIGH ST. STARTING 8·00pm.

▶Starting an action group

The initiative for Macclesfield Women's Aid and Feltham Community Association emerged through personal contacts and friendships. The Macclesfield county councillor contacted people whom he knew shared his concern for victims of family violence. In Feltham, friends and trade unionists got together to tackle the lack of social and welfare facilities in the area.

In the cases of the Sickle Cell Society and the St Helens & District Handicapped Children's Trust, the initiative was taken by workers in the health profession who sought to bring together patients and colleagues to tackle the problems of isolation and confusion experienced by the patients and their families.

However your idea for voluntary and community action arises, your first step will be to try and make contact with others who feel the same way as you. You may also want to find out more about the issue you intend to tackle.

Some people who will be able to help you with this are:

● community workers and information officers at your local council.

● your local librarian.

● members and staff of your local Community Health Council, Council for Voluntary Service, Rural Community Council and Community Association.

How to make contact with these people is described in Chapter 12, 'Resources'. It also includes a list of national organisations who will be able to advise you on a wide range of matters relevant to voluntary and community groups. They may also be able to put you in touch with individuals or groups in your area. If they're not able to help you themselves, they will be able to put you in contact with someone who can answer your questions.

By now you should have:

■ established there is a need, even if only very loosely defined at this stage, for your idea to be put into practice.

■ made informal contact with several people with a similar concern or interest.

Your next step will be to hold an informal meeting of these interested people to work out more precisely the group's aims and initial plan of action.

Your first meeting

● this may be the first time some people will have met and they will need an opportunity to get to know each other and find out if they want to work together. Although the meeting should be formal in the sense of taking notes and ensuring the matter in hand is discussed properly without too much digression, it is important to balance this with an atmosphere of informality.

● you can hold this meeting in your own home or your local Council for Voluntary Services, or Community Association may be able to provide you with a small meeting room, or tell you where a suitable room can be found.

● make sure everyone who is likely to attend knows of the date, time and place. Also, give them an idea of what the meeting will be about: it should be to work out the aims of the group and to consider how to achieve those aims.
   A useful tip for ensuring the discussion at the meeting remains relevant is to ask each person beforehand to make a list of **their** aims for the group and to bring this with them to the meeting. These lists can form the basis of your discussion.

● at the start of the meeting it is helpful to ask members to introduce themselves and then to ask one person to take the Chair and another to take notes. The chairperson may well be the person who called the meeting so they can start by outlining its purpose and summarising the information they have obtained so far.

● now you begin your 'brainstorming' session. ('Brainstorming' refers to discussions which are totally unstructured.) People put forward their aims for the group. However unrelated they may appear to other ideas under discussion, they should all be given serious consideration and accepted or rejected for good reasons. From this the real aims of the group will become apparent.
   Whilst you want people to talk freely during the session, the chairperson should ensure that everyone has an opportunity to say what they feel about the issue and to go through their list of aims. The chairperson should not dominate the meeting

however. You must also take notes. They need not be a verbatim account but simply a summary of the decisions made at the meeting.

● when choosing a name for your group bear in mind the following points:
  ● keep it simple
  ● imagine how it will look in print
  ● consider how it will be abbreviated – avoid initials which spell out a word you would prefer not to be known by!
  ● make sure the name reflects the image you want to convey

● your next job is to plan your initial action. In most cases this will take the form of making the public aware of your existence. The most common method is to hold a public meeting to launch the campaign.

What a mixed bag!

New members East Ardsley Community Council near Wakefield, have published a list of topics they dealt with last year. They include parking problems, water supply, grass verges, listed buildings, an old colliery site, footpaths, bus time tables, telephone kiosks, community policemen, speeding traffic, street nameplates, re-opening a railway station, working on an official General Improvement Area, a gala, firework display, a play project, starting a building fund, launching six clubs and working with Social Services on care schemes for the sick and disabled.

from "Community" Spring 1982

Other situations may require more research, such as a count of the number of houses left vacant in a town, or a survey of the wishes of tenants for social and educational facilities on their estate. Often the two methods go together. Either it is agreed at the public meeting that an extensive survey be carried out, followed by another public meeting to make known your findings or the small informal group decides to undertake the research on their own and present their findings at their first public meeting as a way of launching their campaign.

- balance formality with informality so people can get to know each other.

- make sure everyone knows the date, time and place of the meeting.

- ask people to make a list of their aims for the group before the meeting.

- ask one person to chair the meeting and another to take notes.

- draw up a list of the aims and objectives for the group.

- plan your initial action.

▷Working out your objectives

● **objectives and aims are statements of your intentions.** It is essential you have a clear idea of what you are hoping to achieve before you launch your campaign publicly.

● **objectives should be reviewed frequently** as the campaign or project develops to see whether you are in fact making progress towards meeting the need you have identified. For example, the Earlstown Opportunity Playgroup began with the intention of arranging a playgroup solely for handicapped children. They went on to include socially deprived children in the group because it emerged that they also needed this type of facility. So their objectives changed over time. And they may change again in the future if they are successful in opening their Children's Centre.

● **failure to analyse your objectives at the beginning can lead to problems later.** It sometimes happens that members of an apparently strong and thriving voluntary group disband because they suddenly become aware that they each want the group to achieve different things. This was the experience of Macclesfield Women's Aid. The objective seemed simple – to find a building. Subsequently, different views and objectives emerged about the way a Refuge for battered women should be run. Similarly, the Sickle Cell Society came to feel their objectives were not the same as those of the members of OSCAR.

● a list of objectives is necessary if you intend applying for charitable status.

● a list of objectives is a useful aid to publicising your campaign: it helps avoid misrepresentation about who you are and what you are trying to achieve.

● objectives are also a useful tool for a chairperson who is trying to keep the group together on a united course of action. It makes it possible for him or her to say: "I'm afraid that's not what we're about. We agreed to set up a community centre, not a vehicle repair shop."

The examples of constitutions set out at the end of this book all have a list of objectives at the beginning. Have a look at these now to see how they are phrased. Also, if you are intending to apply for charitable status, please read Chapter 4 to ensure at this early stage that your objectives meet the requirements of the Charity Commission.

■ draw up a list of objectives for your group, keeping them broad and flexible to cover every foreseeable situation.

■ if you want to obtain charitable status make sure these objectives comply with the Charity Commission's rules.

■ review your objectives frequently – are they still relevant, or do you need to change them to reflect the group's work more accurately?

▶How to carry out research

Well-researched reports are a useful tool in any campaign. The bureaucratic reply to many pressure groups, local and national, is "You prove it". You can anticipate that response by having the facts and figures at your fingertips. Good research also helps you clarify your own attitude towards the issue and may highlight aspects which had not occurred to you before. So although it may seem tedious, it is well worth the effort in the end.

Planning your research

Begin by asking yourselves:

● what information do you require?
● how can you best obtain that information?

Example:

You are planning a campaign against the number of houses left vacant on your estate for long periods of time.

You will need to decide:
● whether 'houses' includes flats, maisonettes, bed-sits? Only council houses? Or only privately-owned or rented houses? Or all of these?
● how long is a "long period of time"? - 3 weeks, 6 months, 2 or 5 years?

You will need to know:
● the address of each property
● the length of time each property has been empty
● the reasons for this
● who owns the property
● whether there are any proposals for its occupation in the future
● the condition of the property - is it habitable?
● its approximate size - is it a family dwelling? Elderly person's bed-sit?

To obtain this information you will need to:
● do a house-to-house survey, completing a questionnaire for each empty house.
● interview officials at the local housing and planning departments, as well as other individuals or organisations such as neighbours, estate agents and so on.
● refer to various documents such as Council minutes about road proposals, planning applications etc.

Having worked out what information you want and how to obtain it, you will need to divide the tasks amongst the group. Obviously, if a member of the group has a particular skill, you should allocate them the task which requires that specialist knowledge. Similarly, take account of any special difficulties some members may have. A women with two or three children of pushchair age would have difficulty doing a door-to-door survey in a block of high-rise flats.

One person should be appointed to co-ordinate the research,

making sure everyone does their bit and sorting out any problems which may arise.

Methods of research

Questionnaires

This is the most suitable method for obtaining the views of a large number of people. Here are some hints for designing questionnaires:–

● try to keep to multiple-choice questions 'Tick the appropriate box.' This makes it easier to collate the results.

● present an even number of answers otherwise 90% of your respondents may well tick the middle box – fair, medium, sometimes!

● try to avoid absurd answers. Check the relevance of your questions by asking a friend who has no involvement in your campaign to complete the form.

● be aware of the bias of respondents and don't be disappointed if there is a poor response to your questionnaire – 10% is a good response. Some people fill in every form and coupon which drops through their letterbox. Most people only fill in those which are about an issue very close to their hearts.

● how will people complete the questionnaire? Will members of the group call on local people and complete it with them or will the forms be put through letterboxes for people to return themselves? The level of response and degree of bias will be affected by whichever method you choose. People tend to answer more fully and present a stronger viewpoint when they are interviewed personally.

Big demand for centre

Linthorpe CA, near Middlesbrough, have conducted a survey of local opinion. An astonishing 70% of the questionnaires were returned and 96% of them wanted a community centre in the area. The one problem they do face is that the area straddles the boundary of our Inner City programme area – and any new centre will only qualify for assistance if it is inside the boundary.

from "Community" Summer 1982

Interviews

Interviews are fine if you don't have to get the views of a large number of people. They are a good method for obtaining the views of officials, such as the manager of the housing department or social workers who may be reluctant to fill in forms but are prepared to discuss the matter with you in the sanctuary of their office. In any case, it is always a good idea to make an appointment to talk to any local officials whose work will have a bearing on your campaign. This may help establish a good working relationship in the future.

Prepare a list of questions and at the end of the interview check that all the points on your list have been answered, not necessarily in the order of your list, but during the course of the conversation. Ask the interviewee if you can take notes. Only take them if they agree! If they disagree, write down your thoughts about the meeting as soon as possible afterwards as important details can be quickly forgotten. Always follow up the interview with a short note to thank them and to confirm the main points of the discussion.

Written sources of information

National statistics are useful for comparison and analysis. For example, it may not be practical for you to attempt to forecast the number of people who will be diagnosed as having chronic heart disease in your locality in the next ten years. But you could take national medical statistics on which to form a well-educated guess and then check that there are no special reasons why your area should vary from the norm. For example there may be an above average number of people over the age of 60 in your town. You will have to refer to local population statistics at your library or council offices.

Always make a note of your source of information and quote this in your research paper so others can go to the library and check it for themselves. This will counteract any claims that you dreamt up the figure.

Presenting your research

Some points to bear in mind:

● always make your final report attractive – neatly typed in double spacing, adequate margins and a front page with just the title, date and name of the organisation.

● when writing up your report, think about who will read it and adjust your style accordingly. Avoid jargon!

● prepare a summary of your report, say 2-4 pages long. You may prefer to circulate this summary widely and ask people to contact you if they would like a copy of the complete report. Editors of local newspapers do not usually have enough staff available to wade through 60-page reports in order to find a few electrifying statistics which they can quote – often out of context. So, if you want publicity which reflects the image you want, it helps to do the work for them by sending a summary and asking them to contact you for further information.

 ■ list the information you require.

■ decide how you can best obtain this information.

■ allocate tasks to members of the group.

■ appoint one person to co-ordinate the research.

■ take care with the presentation of your report.

■ write a summary of your report.

▷Your first public meeting

Most of the points presented here apply to all public meetings. Chapter 5 looks at the roles of the chairperson and secretary, how to draw up an agenda, take minutes and so on. You may find it helpful to glance quickly through that chapter after reading this section.

Begin by thinking about the purpose of your public meeting and ask yourself the following questions:

Who do you want to attend?

If you are setting up a Community Association, for example, you will want local people to attend, as well as councillors and representatives of other local organisations. This determines the date, time and place of your meeting. As many of these people will be at work during the day an evening meeting will probably be more convenient. They are unlikely to appreciate a meeting at the weekend. Does the date you've chosen clash with any other big event? Check what's on TV – avoid clashing with coverage of important football matches or Royal Weddings! Give people an opportunity to have something to eat between getting home from work and coming out to your meeting – unless you're providing substantial refreshments.

On the other hand, if you want to attract mothers to your meeting the day time would be better. Avoid times when they are likely to be taking children to and from school. Ensure the meeting place can be easily reached by public transport, or is within walking distance.

What will happen at the meeting?

If you want the meeting to make decisions about the future of the group, it is helpful to draft resolutions beforehand. You may also want endorsement of your informal group as the executive committee of the organisation, in which case it helps to have nominations lined up so that there are no ghastly silences. Similarly, you may want to arrange for the nomination of other people who could be useful to the organisation – your local MP could become honorary president of the association.

Do you want a speaker?

Decide whether you want a speaker or well-known local personality to open the meeting. Check that they are available before you book the meeting room or start your publicity. Do you know of any other people who would be suitable for opening the meeting if the person of your first choice is booked for months ahead? A speaker adds interest to the meeting and attracts more people as well as greater publicity.

Will you want to have further public meetings?

If you anticipate that the people at this meeting will agree to certain action being taken it is likely they will want to know the outcome of that action. It is vital to involve other people from the start if you are to avoid being seen as a clique and wear yourself out by having to do all the work yourself. If you think another meeting will be necessary, have some suitable dates in mind so people can make a note of them before they leave.

How will you pay for the meeting?

A few local councils will make 'starter' grants to local voluntary and community groups, usually of about £50. Some national voluntary organisations also have start-up funds for their new local branches, of about the same amount.

Otherwise you will probably have to meet the costs of the first public meeting yourself. As you will want to keep these to a minimum, you should approach your local CVS or RCC to see whether they can provide or obtain a meeting room on your behalf free of charge, or try your local community centre. You could make a small charge for the refreshments or ask your audience for a contribution to costs. Avoid expensive newspaper advertisements. Ask them to print an article instead. Contact your local CVS or RCC to see whether they can print leaflets and posters cheaply for you.

Obtain receipts for all the monies you pay out so that if, later on, you receive substantial donations you can repay yourselves for those expenses. Chapter 6 tells you how to keep account of all the group's money.

Will there be refreshments?

A cup of tea and a biscuit either before or after the meeting is an excellent way of strengthening people's commitment to a project!

Always try to end your meeting on a note of hope – the problem you're intending to tackle will be solved with the support of those attending the meeting. Make them feel necessary to the success of the group so they will want to remain involved.

Other points to remember about your first public meeting:

● **always obtain the names and addresses of those present** and the capacity in which they are attending – are they a local headteacher, policeman, councillor?

● **take notes of the main points raised at the meeting** and of any resolutions. These notes should be typed up afterwards and either circulated in that form to those who came to the meeting, or a summary made and circulated. Examples of minutes of meetings are contained in Chapter 5.

● **always send out a follow-up of some sort** – either the summarised notes referred to above or a letter a few weeks later telling people how the campaign is progressing. You should at least send them a short note thanking them for attending the meeting with a promise to keep them informed of developments.

● **be sure to aim your publicity** at those you want to attract to the meeting and give ample notice of the meeting.

● **your local CVS or RCC** may be able to give you any further advice you need with organising your public meeting.

● **Try to appoint** one person to co-ordinate all the arrangements.

- choose a date, time and place convenient for the people you want to attend.
- draft resolutions beforehand.
- check that your speaker is available before you publicise the meeting.
- check whether your local council makes 'starter' grants.
- plan your publicity carefully, bearing in mind the people you want to come to the meeting.
- end your meeting on a note of hope and optimism.
- obtain names and addresses of people who attend and keep in touch with them.
- take notes of any decisions which are made at the meeting.
- appoint one person to co-ordinate all the arrangements for the meeting.

4 GETTING ORGANISED

▷ Do you want to become a charity?
▷ The advantages of charitable status
▷ How do you become a charity?
▷ Which charities are exempt from registration?
▷ What is a constitution?
▷ Other legal forms

ON A CLEAR DAY YOU CAN SEE .... AT LEAST HALF A DOZEN FUNDING ORGANISATIONS ...

▷ Do you want to become a charity?

Today's law relating to charities dates back to the 17th century and not unnaturally it has come to be regarded as out of date and restrictive, particularly in view of the growth of the new style community and pressure groups. But despite constant lobbying by the voluntary sector, there have been no substantial changes and the small advances which have been achieved are the result of individual organisations' appeals through the courts.

Nearly 2,000 organisations register as charities every year. Most of these are small local groups.

▷ The advantages of charitable status

Advantages	Disadvantages
Helps with fund-raising from the general public, trusts and industry	Limits political and campaigning activity
Entitlement to at least 50% rate relief	Subject to monitoring by the Charity Commission

Entitlement to tax relief on:
    – corporation tax
    – capital transfer tax
    – national insurance
 (see Chapter 6)
	Takes time to register
	
	 Limits trading activity

The prime reason for seeking charitable status is financial. It is a yardstick by which an organisation is judged to be entitled to certain financial benefits, much as unemployment is a yardstick for measuring an individual's entitlement to state welfare benefits. Charitable status also confers respectability making it easier for organisations to raise money from public and private sources.

What is a charity not allowed to do?

● **political campaigning or anything which reflects a political stance. Nor must it aim to change any laws.** Limited political activity will only be permitted if it is necessary for fulfilment of the charity's aims, but there is a very thin line between what is permitted and what is not. One way of getting around this problem is to establish a separate organisation with an indisputable charitable function which can claim the tax and other benefits, leaving the parent organisation without charity status but free to pursue its political activities. The National Council for Civil Liberties, for example, established its subsidiary, the Cobden Trust, as a charity.

● **trading which makes a profit or becomes a mainstream activity of the group.** Again, the way round this problem is to establish a separate organisation for trading, with all profits being donated back to the charity. This procedure was adopted by Feltham Community Association who set up a non-charitable social club to look after the licenced bar, the profits from which were then covenanted back to the Association.

Normal fund-raising events are permitted so long as all profits are used for charitable purposes.

▷How do you become a charity?

Do you have to use a solicitor?

No. Unless you know of one who will do the work for you free of charge, or at a reduced cost, it can be an expensive process. There are several excellent books on the subject, however, and some of these are listed in Chapter 12 'Resources'. Many groups prefer to do the job themselves, with the aid of a local community worker, or their local Council for Voluntary Service, or a parent national organisation. The Charity Commissioners will also advise you.

When should you start the registration process?

Registration has been known to take as long as two years! But normally you can expect it to take between six months and a year. It is easier for a group which is still in the formation stages to obtain charitable status, preferably before your activities have been publicised. The reason for this is that the local press reports may distort the aims of your organisation so they appear to the Charity Commissioners to be political.

Who are the trustees and what are their responsibilities?

The basis of charitable status is that there is a trust. The charity trustees are those who have management and control of the funds of the trust. If the status of the organisation rests simply upon a trust deed, then the charity's trustees are the trustees mentioned in the deed. If there is a constitution, the charity trustees are those having control under that constitution, normally the Management Committee or General meeting. If the organisation is incorporated under the Companies Acts, then it is the directors who are the charity trustees; if it is registered under the Industrial and Provident Societies Acts, the trustees are the committee.

For the sake of continuity, it may be decided to vest the trust property in custodian or holding trustees, a corporation, such as a bank or insurance company, or the Official Custodian. The latter is a government department and does not charge for its services and the vesting is accomplished by a simple form.

The holding, or custodian, trustees do not manage the trust property. They simply hold the documents of title and under the direction of the managing trustees, lease, sell or license it. If these trustees are incorporated they have 'perpetual succession' and there is no need to draw up deeds of appointment when a trustee dies, or retires.

Neither type of trustee can receive remuneration for their work on behalf of the charity, other than reimbursement of expenses. This means that the staff you employ cannot be made trustees. The only exceptions to this rule of non-payment are professional trustees such as solicitors and auditors who are entitled to make charges for the work they do on behalf of the charity.

Will charitable status automatically give you the right to claim all the financial benefits?

No. When the Charity Commissioners are considering an application for charitable status they consult the Inland Revenue who tend to take a tougher line about what is a charitable activity. Although the Charity Commission may suggest some amendments to the applicant's constitution to get round the Inland Revenue's objections, the latter may still refuse to give tax relief if it feels the income of the charity is not being used for charitable purposes.

Local authorities, on the other hand, will accept charitable status as automatic entitlement to rate relief, and it is usually sufficient to satisfy the needs of grant-making trusts.

Lifting the lid on the charity laws

Voluntary Action **reports on tax reform, plans for modernising the charity laws, a test case in the courts and of course, Penlee.**

Penlee: Treasury giveaway worth 'virtually nothing'

The Government gave away 'virtually nothing' in its highly publicised tax concession to the trustees of the Penlee lifeboat fund, says the solicitor to the Cornish district council which launched the spectacular fund. And the Home Office has turned down pleas for a review of the law surrounding charitable giving.

When the fund for the families affected by the lifeboat tragedy closed, it contained around £2.7 million. This will be divided between the dependants of the eight men who died – a capital sum of around £330,000 for each family. There will probably be an annual income before tax, of roughly £30,000 for each family.

The row over the money began when the trustees of the Penwith District Council disaster fund investigated the implications of registering the fund as a charity. They learned that a charity would only be allowed to give the dependants as much money as they needed to maintain their previous lifestyle. But it seemed that if the fund was established as an ordinary private trust, a hefty proportion of the wellwishers' money would be snapped up by the Inland Revenue as the gifts of money became subject to capital transfer tax.

The main outcry centred around the 'bureaucrats, lawyers, do-gooders and tax collectors', all of whom, as *The Times* pointed out, were seen as getting in the way between the givers and the Penlee families. In the glare of publicity, almighty confusion reigned for a week or two.

Eventually, as Mr Rowland, Penwith District Council's solicitor explained to *Voluntary Action*, a private trust was established, though without a formal trust deed. The trustees will parcel up the money into eight shares.

An obscure clause in the 1975 Finance Act was discovered, which provides a loophole through which the families can avoid paying capital transfer tax on their windfalls. However this loophole,' which owes nothing to Government generosity, does not apply to any tax liability on the part of the *donors* of large sums. In a gesture of goodwill, the Chancellor of the Exchequer conceded that capital transfer tax would not be levied on large donations to the Penlee fund (ie individual gifts of more than £3000). Mr Rowland commented, 'the concession looked very good at the time, but we've had very few large donations and so it is worth virtually nothing'.

The concession stands on its own and is not a precedent for any similar funds in the future. Now the Attorney General is preparing guidance for appeal organisers, giving alternative formulae on which funds can be based.

from "Voluntary Action" Spring 1982

What is the position for organisations in Scotland and Northern Ireland?

Only groups in England and Wales need to be registered with the Charity Commission. Prospective charities in Scotland and Northern Ireland have to obtain the approval of the Inland Revenue who will send you a letter confirming your acceptance as a charity.

The process for obtaining this acceptance, however, is largely the same as that of registration with the Charity Commission for English and Welsh groups.

What is a 'charity'?

To become a registered charity, the objectives of your group will have to fit into one of the following four categories:–

● **relief of poverty** – even if you are providing benefit to only a small group of people, such as widows of servicemen or children of single parents in your town, you can be accepted for registration under this heading.

● **advancement of education** – this does not refer only to academic teaching. Most organisations seeking to inform the public of social developments try to obtain charitable status under this heading. As Denis Peach, the new chief Charity Commissioner said in an interview for the magazine, Voluntary Action, "Just write in the magic word 'education' and it's alright."

● **advancement of religion** – this is taken to mean 'the promotion of spiritual teaching in a wide sense' so the organisation must have an open membership: an enclosed order of nuns or monks does not qualify – the Moonies do!

● **other purposes beneficial to the community** – wildlife and bird protection, conservation, work with ex-offenders and alcoholics are just some of the examples permitted under this clause. But it is not a bandwagon for all good causes – the aims of the organisation must be beneficial to a substantial part of the community it serves.

● **PLEASE REMEMBER:** POLITICAL AND TRADING OBJECTIVES ARE NOT PERMITTED

Lobbying

Overheard at a recent voluntary organisation get-together: 'Oh, we never have any trouble with the Charity Commission, and we're up to our necks in political campaigning. What we do is ask our friends in Parliament to request that we send them information on a particular issue, Bill going through Parliament, or whatever. When we get their letters, we tell them our point of view, but that way no-one can accuse us of lobbying'. Neat.

from "Voluntary Action" Spring 1982

HOW DO YOU OBTAIN CHARITABLE STATUS?

■ **send the Charity Commission a copy of your constitution in draft form.** Also, send them an outline of your activities making sure these tie in with your objectives and that they are non-political. They will send back comments on your draft and you can make the amendments required by them.

■ **call a general meeting of the group to endorse that constitution** when the Charity Commission is satisfied with your draft.

■ **make formal application to the Charity Commission** for registration on form RE1. Enclose your finalised constitution together with any trust deeds or Company Articles of Association, if these apply, and information about the trustees and the organisation's activities.

■ **if your application is successful** you will be given a registration number. You can quote this on your notepaper and publicity material.

■ **if your application is not successful you can appeal** against the decision. If that appeal fails you can appeal through the courts. You will not be entitled to legal aid, however, so this can be an expensive business.

■ **each year** you will have to submit to the Charity Commission a copy of your Annual Report and Accounts, minutes of the Annual General Meeting and details of any new trustees – name, address, age and occupation.

Charity Law - Is this the limit?

by Bevan Jones

Charity law has been causing concern to a great many voluntary organisations - not just community groups. But, as described in an earlier issue of COMMUNITY, the Charity Commission in recent years appears to have been scrutinising community groups applying for registration with particular care.

Inevitably, NFCO has been drawn into the issues arising from this scrutiny. At the simplest level, we have had to respond to members demoralised by a legalistic broadside from the Charity Commission. For a small group of volunteers attempting to improve their daily lives on a new housing estate an official list of objections to their activities can be a deeply alarming experience. Most such activities are entirely worthy and often represent achievements of which the organisation is justifiably proud.

But worthiness is not necessarily charitable. A self-help body may be worthy, but it lacks the element of public benefit essential for charitable status.

Why are some organisations picked on and not others? Firstly, new organisations applying for charitable status are being more closely scrutinised. In the case of community associations this seems to be due in part to the broad objectives of their constitution. It seems usual for the Charity Commission to ask for clarification, often in the form of newsletters, reports and so on.

Care should be taken to ensure that any material sent to the Commission accurately reflects charitable purposes. Secondly, existing organisations may be called to account because the Commission has learnt of questionable activity. This may result from the Commission's routine scrutiny of reports and accounts or from complaints made to the Commission.

But beyond these problems lies the question of just how a voluntary group interprets its constitution in a manner consistent with common sense - and stays within the boundaries of charity law. It must be said that the common sense understanding of the word 'charitable' is much broader than its legal definition.

To examine this question adequately it is important to understand the basic framework under which charities in England and Wales operate. Put at its most basic, charities are voluntary organisations given legal recognition and privileges by the State.

These privileges are substantial. Charities are exempt from taxes such as corporation and income tax - though not, sadly, VAT - and receive mandatory rate relief on their premises. They also attract almost automatic public sympathy and respectability and can receive grants from other charities.

Legal requirements

However, to achieve charitable status the organisation has to comply with certain legal requirements. These include public accountability, defined trustees, a dissolution procedure but, above all, the organisation's objectives must conform to what legally is charitable. This is where the complications set in. The law classifies charities under four headings: religion, education, the relief of poverty and sickness - and certain other purposes deemed 'beneficial to the community'.

Since charity law dates back to 1601, the body of case law is considerable. The disadvantage of this is revealed by the two main areas of current contention. The first is the problem of 'new' causes: human rights, race relations, unemployment are all seen as outside the scope of charity law. The second contentious area is political action by charities. This is one of the crunch points and is an area where the Charity Commission has been zealous

38

of late.   Concern has also been voiced by Government ministers.

Most community groups have their origins in a desire to improve the quality of local life.   This can mean a whole host of different things to different communities and their different needs.   A neighbourhood with a lot of pensioners will probably want social events and outings, as well as education classes.   An inner city area may well be concerned with housing, race relations and traffic.   A new estate will want to promote neighbourliness and keep an eye on planning matters.   Some of these activities can provoke objections from the Charity Commission if it is not made clear that the activity was furthering a charitable object.   Thus, a seaside outing to help the housebound or to educate young people about seaside fauna is charitable while one for pleasure only is questionable.

Local authority

Taking an interest in matters relating to the quality of life - even such mundane issues as the siting of a pedestrian crossing - can be construed as political, especially if you try to persuade your local authority to take action.

NFCO has now discussed these difficulties with Dennis Peach, the Chief Charity Commissioner.   Happily, there is a willingness for NFCO and the Commission to work together and resolve any problems which arise. The guidance now offered is much clearer and should reassure many of NFCO's members.

Roughly speaking, the Charity Commission says that any activity which could be construed as political must arise out of the performance of your charitable purposes i.e. it must be in furtherance of the objects clause of your constitution.   It must not be associated with any political party and it has to be a minor part of

your activity.   It must not campaign for a change in the law or in national or local government policy.   The style in which campaigns are conducted is important - they must be reasoned expressions of opinion backed up by your experience of operating as a charity.

Grey area

So, three principles now govern what was a grey area. One, activities must be justified in terms of your original charitable objects. Two, they must not be political in the sense described above.   Three, the more strident in style and tone the campaign is, the more likely it is to be construed as political.

Should a community group decide that a full-blooded campaign is the only course open to them, then the answer is to set up a distinct campaign committee. It may well be the association under another hat but it must have a separate identity and must not be able to use the charitable resources - principally money - of the parent charity.

The advice NFCO now gives to its membership is straightforward: refer to the objects clause of your constitution.   Interpret what you do in the light of these objects.   Consult the Charity Commission if you are unsure about the boundaries around you.

For its part, the Charity Commission has undertaken to be more accessible and sympathetic in its dealings with NFCO's membership. For our part, NFCO hopes that its members will recognise the sense of the guidelines described in this article and will be able to get on with their job of building better communities as they have been doing for most of this century.

NFCO will shortly publish an Information Sheet on the subject "Charitable Status and Registration" - order no. 82.

from 'Community' Autumn 1983

39

▷Which charities are exempt from registration?

The main exemptions are:

● Boy Scouts and Girl Guides.

● Church of England bodies, Baptist, Congregational and other churches, and places of worship.

● societies registered under the Industrial and Provident Societies Act or the Friendly Societies Act.

● voluntary schools.

● small charities with less than £15 income a year and without any property.

▷What is a constitution?

As soon as a group of people get together to work on a joint activity, they have formed an organisation. The basis of the organisation will be the constitution, and you will be deemed by the courts to have one whether or not it is written down.

The constitution sets out the aims of the group, the ways in which it will achieve those aims and the way the group is structured and managed.

Here are some points to bear in mind when drawing up your constitution:

● **make it flexible** and broad enough to cope with all the situations you can envisage at the time it is written. For example, if it is your long-term intention to establish a community centre even though you have no funds or prospect of any funds with which to do so at this stage, you should still make some reference to it in your 'Objects clause'. 'To establish or to secure the establishment of a community centre...'

● **beware of ambiguities and anomalies.** For example, if you define several classes of membership will they all have equal voting rights? Or do you need to specify which classes have which type of voting rights?

● **the constitution should reflect the style of your organisation.** Do you want a hierarchical structure with considerable power vested in the Executive or the chairperson, or do you want to maximise participation by ordinary members? Consider carefully what powers you delegate and to which part of the organisation, and try to imagine how particular situations will be dealt with in practice.

● **if you use a 'model' constitution** provided by a parent or national organisation which has acquired charitable status for itself on the basis of that constitution, you must not alter the 'Objects' clause in any way whatsoever. Even a small amendment may cause your application to be unsuccessful. There have been a number of such cases recently. Charitable status granted to a parent organisation does not extend to its local branches who must each make a separate application.

Here are the basic clauses to include in your constitution. You may require others to meet the needs of your particular organisation. Even if you do not wish to become a charity the following notes will give you a guide to the points your constitution should cover.

The name of the association

The objects

Here you list the aims and objectives of your group. Remember this is the clause which causes problems with the Charity Commission – so be careful!

Membership

You can have individual and/or group members and both types can be divided again into various classes of membership.

● **individual members** – state whether there are any characteristics required for membership, such as age, sex, place of residence, and what classes of membership are available – full, junior, associate, life.

● **group members** – many organisations, such as Feltham Community Association, like to have the option of including representatives of other local voluntary groups in their membership. Some organisations' membership is comprised entirely of other groups, like Councils for Voluntary Service. 'Groups' can also include your local authority or other statutory agencies with whom you want to work closely.

41

● **co-opted members** – are there people with a special knowledge or interest in the work of your group who cannot meet the requirements for ordinary membership? If so, you can co-opt them under a general clause such as 'The Council may co-opt further persons who shall become members of the Association...'. You should state what is the maximum proportion of co-options to the general membership – usually it is one-third – and whether these people should seek re-appointment at intervals. If you do not stipulate a need for re-appointment you may find yourself stuck with people whose usefulness has expired and whose number exceeds the proportion you have set for co-opted members. Generally speaking, you should think carefully about co-opting members – it can be difficult to refuse re-appointment to someone who has been involved with the organisation for a long time. It may be better to invite the person to become an adviser to your group on matters relating to their special interest or knowledge. This meets your needs for flexibility and fosters good public relations as well as giving that person an opportunity to participate in the organisation.

● **applications for membership** – most organisations require that applications be approved either by the Executive or by a meeting of the full membership. This prevents infiltration by any undesirable groups, such as extremist political groups.

● **termination of membership** – a clause about termination of membership may also be necessary unless membership depends on the fulfilment of certain criteria and termination is automatic if the criteria no longer apply. For example, a person reaching 26 years of age is no longer a member of a club for 18-25 year-olds, unless you have another class of membership, associate membership for example, enabling long-standing members to remain involved with the club.

Subscription

Here you should either state the exact membership fee or include a general clause such as 'All members and constituents shall pay such subscriptions as the Council may from time to time determine.'

The Council

The term used to refer to the heart of the organisation –

usually it comprises all the members plus any co-opted persons. It is the policy and decision-making body of the organisation. Normally the Council will appoint an Executive or Management Committee to carry out the day-to-day work of the organisation, although the Council retains the right to override decisions made by that or any other Committees it decides to appoint.

The Executive Committee

Manages the organisation's day-to-day affairs but is always responsible to the Council. You should list the powers delegated to it by the Council. Usually these include appointment of staff, sub-committees and representatives to outside organisations. Decide how many people you want on your Executive Committee – between 6 and 15 is the norm, depending on the size of the organisation – and how they will be selected. No doubt you will want your Executive to be representative of the different views and interest groups within the Council, but not so large as to be unwieldy.

General Meeting

How often will the Council meet? It must meet at least once a year for the Annual General Meeting at which the honorary officers and the Executive Committee will be elected, and the Annual Accounts and Report presented. The length of notice given for General meetings should be stipulated – 21 days is the standard – and how the notice will be given – in writing, by advertisement in the local paper – and the number of members required to be present for the meeting to be quorate.

Special General Meetings

Under what conditions can a Special meeting be called, and how will it be called?

Executive Meetings

How often will the Executive meet, how will meetings be called, and what will be the quorum?

Appointment of officers

In this context 'officers' refers to the honorary – unpaid – positions of chairperson, treasurer and secretary. If your organisation employs staff you may want to appoint your most senior member to be the secretary. Their other job is to ensure that the work is carried out and continuity maintained. If your group is a company, the secretary will become the company secretary responsible for all the legalities involved in being a company. If the secretary is a staff member she or he will also become an ex-officio – non-voting – member of the Executive.

Honorary appointments are made at the Annual General Meeting. If there are mid-term resignations it is usual for the Executive to have the power to appoint a replacement from amongst their membership for the remainder of the year.

Normally the chairperson of the Council is also chairperson of the Executive Committee but some organisations prefer to have a figurehead as chairperson of the Council with a title like honorary president, and someone actively involved as chairperson. The treasurer is sometimes a co-opted member or adviser – perhaps a local accountant who has offered services free of charge and doesn't qualify for ordinary membership, or a finance officer of the local authority.

Procedure at meetings

This section of your constitution should cover voting – who, when, how, the casting vote – the size of quorum, and who will record the minutes.

Standing Orders

These are a set of rules for conducting business at meetings, that is, how resolutions should be presented, seconded, amended and so on. It is usual for these to be separate from the constitution, which simply makes reference to them. Frequently, the Executive Committee is given the power to draw up Standing Orders for approval and periodic review by the Council.

Accounts

This clause covers the appointment of auditors and the manner in which accounts should be kept.

Dissolution

You must state under what circumstances the organisation can be wound up and how dissolution will take place. It is also necessary to say what will happen to any property or funds in the organisation's ownership. A registered charity has to donate any excess funds to another charity with objects similar to its own.

Alterations to the constitution

Who has the right to propose an alteration? How much notice is required? If you are a registered charity all proposed alterations, in particular the Objects clause, must first have the approval of the Charity Commission.

Two examples of constitutions are printed at the end of this book. These vary in complexity and include clauses other than those listed above.

If you intend doing the job yourself, it may be helpful to start by appointing a small group of members – say 2 to 6 – to go through these examples, 'lifting' those clauses which are relevant, and work out a skeleton for your constitution. Your local CVS or RCC will probably have other examples for you to look at. They will be able to advise you on any changes which may be required for your group.

▷Other legal forms

The first thing is to decide whether you want to be an **unincorporated** organisation. This approach makes named individuals legally responsible for the conduct of the organisation. Perhaps you want to be an **incorporated** organisation, which means the group has a legal identity of its own, separate from its members

Forms of unincorporated organisations are:
● unincorporated associations, societies or clubs
● trusts
● Friendly Societies

Forms of incorporated organisations are:
● limited companies
● Industrial and Provident Societies

Unincorporated associations, societies or clubs

These are not usually charitable organisations as they tend to exist primarily for the benefit of their members, as opposed to the community.

Charitable trusts

Trusts are most commonly used where property is involved. It is a simple legal agreement between three people, or groups. The first, the donor, agrees with the second, the trustees, to give them property which they will hold for the benefit of the third, the beneficiaries. The needs of the beneficiaries must be acceptable to the Charity Commissioners and the Inland Revenue for the trust to be regarded as charitable and so entitled to financial benefits.

The advantages of a trust are that the deeds can be easily amended and it does not have to be registered with any public body. It is cheap to establish and there are no registration fees or taxes to pay. A serious disadvantage, however, is that the trustees are named persons and cannot be changed without drawing up a new deed of appointment. Another disadvantage is that trustees have personal financial liability for any breach of the trust or debts incurred under the trust, so they are necessarily cautious about what they permit the beneficiaries to do with the property. Because the trustees cannot be changed under the existing deed except by a court, sometimes there is friction between the two parties.

Friendly Societies

These were popular in the last century when voluntary self-help groups were established to relieve poverty amongst their members. Despite its simplicity and cheapness it is not a form used by many community and voluntary groups today as the objects of a Friendly Society are limited to the mutual relief of hardship. Friendly Societies can obtain all the financial benefits of a charity without having to register with the Charity Commission.

Industrial and Provident Societies (IPS)

An IPS does not need to register with the Charity Commission in order to obtain financial benefits, although it must satisfy the Inland Revenue as to its charitable purposes. Instead, like a Friendly Society, it is subject to monitoring by the Registry of Friendly Societies. An IPS offers the advantage to members of incorporated status, but its purpose has to be for carrying on an industry, business or trade, **and** either be a co-operative or be conducted for the benefit of the community. It is rare for community groups to become an IPS unless they wish to trade.

For example, the Feltham Resources Centre is a co-operative whose profits are donated back to the Association.

Limited companies

There are several forms of limited company. Two common examples are:

● where liability is limited to the amount of a member's share capital.

● where liability is limited to an amount subscribed by members as a guarantee.

The second is known as a 'company whose members' liability is limited by guarantee' and is a popular legal form for community and voluntary groups.

Becoming a company limited by guarantee provides several advantages:

● it gives financial protection to its members and directors.

● it encourages democratic participation by members who can put forward resolutions, vote, and elect officials.

● there is a ready-made constitution known as 'Table C' in the Companies Act of 1948, which organisations can use as the basis of their constitution. Table C sets out arrangements for holding meetings, voting rights and so on. Within limits, it can be altered to meet the particular needs of the organisation.

Setting up a company is a more expensive procedure than establishing a trust although ready-made companies can be purchased through a solicitor for about £100. Alternatively you can establish a new company using your constitution as the basis of your Memorandum and Articles of Association. Either way you will be subject to the Companies Acts of 1948 and 1967 and required to register your company at Companies House annually. A fee is payable each year and you will have to send them a copy of your annual accounts and report, minutes of the A.G.M. and details of any changes in your directors or constitution.

Typically, the members of the organisation pay the appropriate subscription and the Executive, which is elected periodically by those members, becomes the Board of Directors.

Being a Company does not exclude the organisation from also obtaining charitable status, or vice versa. If your organisation is likely to be entering into any significant trading activity or handling large sums of grant aid or other funds, it may well be worth becoming a company as it gives you financial protection as well as flexibility.

- list the benefits which you expect your group to obtain if it were to become a registered charity.

- are these benefits outweighed by the restrictions which will be imposed on the group's activities?

- have you prepared a draft constitution?

- will this be acceptable to the Charity Commission for charitable status?

- are your trustees clear about their responsibilities?

- is limited liability of members important to your group?

Relations with other organisations

Members of your group will probably want to have contact with other voluntary groups in your locality whose work is similar to yours. This may reduce duplication of effort and allow better sharing of information and resources. When required, you may also be able to exert greater pressure on national and local government about issues which affect all the groups or all the groups' clients.

Facilities for liaison may already exist in your area through your local CVS or RCC and you should consider whether you are able to participate in their work. Several CVS's and RCC's have regular meetings with the local authorities to discuss grants, topical issues and other points of mutual concern. If no facility for liaison currently exists in your area, you may consider establishing a forum by calling together representatives of groups involved in work similar to yours. Alternatively, you can co-opt representatives of these groups to your Council or your Executive or both.

Free exchange of information and ideas helps the voluntary sector provide more and better services to the community and helps it adapt to meet changing social needs.

5 MAKING MEETINGS WORK

▷ **Why bother with meetings?**
▷ **The job of the secretary**
▷ **The role of the chairperson**
▷ **How to chair a meeting**

▷Why bother with meetings?

Meetings are an integral part of the work of most voluntary and community groups. All of the organisations featured at the start of this book have had to arrange a variety of meetings to obtain support and funds. They also hold committee meetings, meetings with other voluntary groups, local government officers, and so on.

But if they are poorly managed, meetings are unproductive, expensive and a waste of people's time.

Although there are a few people who love meetings for their own sakes, most of us become frustrated with endless hours of discussion about the same old problems. Voluntary groups depend on the goodwill of everyone involved and a balance has to be achieved between:

● democracy, which allows everyone to vent their feelings, and

● efficiency in reaching clear decisions

The key people for ensuring your meetings are a success are the chairperson and the secretary. They need to work together at all stages of the meeting, from its preparation through to ensuring that the decisions which are made are carried out. Just like the guidelines for public meetings described in Chapter 3, the first tasks of the secretary and chairperson are to decide:

● the purpose of the meeting.

● what matters need to be discussed.

● what the outcome is likely to be, or what outcome is desirable.

You may like to quickly glance back through the relevant section in Chapter 3.

▷The job of the secretary

When organising meetings, the secretary has four main functions:

● **to make all the physical arrangements for the meeting –** booking a suitable room, getting there a little early to check the room is laid out as you wish and that any relevant documents are to hand.

● **to ensure all rules for calling meetings are observed in accordance with the constitution** – length of notice, submission of resolutions etc.

● **to draw up an agenda** – the amount of detail contained in this will vary according to the personality and needs of the group and its members. Here is an example of an agenda:

North Minton Community Association,
Fulshaw House, Minton Green, London

The next meeting of the Executive will be held on 24th April, 7.30pm at Fulshaw House.

Please note, Mr. Bradwell, the Borough Council's architect, will be attending this meeting to dicuss the plans for the new extension and obtaining tenders for the work. It is important, therefore, for everyone to try to attend this meeting.

7.30	1. Apologies for Absence
7.35	2. New Extension – Report from Mr. Bradwell, Borough Council Architect
8.05 approx	3. Minutes of the last meeting held 25th March, copy enclosed
	4. Matters arising from the minutes other than those mentioned elsewhere on this agenda
	5. Arrangements for the A.G.M.
	6. Report on Outing to Southport
	7. Purchase of disco equipment
8.45 approx	8. Treasurer's Report
	9. Fund-raising Committee's Report
	10. Any Other Business – members are requested to inform the Chairman prior to the start of the meeting of any other items they wish to raise at this meeting.

The meeting will close 9.15 – 9.30 approx.

An agenda checklist:

- always state clearly the title of the group or committee which is meeting, and the date, time and place.

- be logical: decide what subjects need to be raised at the meeting and sort out an order of priority for their discussion. Check with members to see if they wish to raise any matters so as to reduce the number of items raised under any other business (AOB).

- if a guest or speaker is attending the meeting give them an early slot.

- avoid being vague: if a matter is sufficiently important to be raised at a meeting it should have its own heading rather than being grouped under 'matters arising' or 'AOB'.

- be informative: describe each item in sufficient detail so members come prepared and interested.

- timing: give an indication of the time to be spent on each item but do not be too rigid.

- enclosures: where practical enclose previous minutes and any written reports so members have an opportunity to read these thoroughly before the meeting.

● to keep minutes of meetings – Here is an example of minutes:

```
            Minutes of a meeting of the North Minton Community Association's
            Executive Committee held 24th April, 7.30pm at Fulshaw House


1.    Members present: Mrs. Cash (Chairperson). Mrs. Arthur,
      Mr. Black, Mrs. Drabble, Mr. Elliot, Mr. Faust
      Guest, Mr. Bradwell, Borough Council Architect

2.    Apologies for Absence: Mr. Webster and Mrs. Drabble

3.    New Extension: Report from Mr. Bradwell, Borough Council
      Architect
            Mr. Bradwell presented the plans for the new extension.
      It was agreed to set up a sub-committee comprising Mrs. Cash,
      Mr. Black and Mrs. Drabble to whom members were asked to
      convey their views of the plans. The sub-committee will pass
      on members' views to Mr. Bradwell during the next two weeks.
            Members received copies of a Borough Council leaflet outling
      the procedure for obtaining tenders. It was agreed the Chairperson,
      Mrs. Cash, should liaise with Mr. Bradwell about the precise
      arrangements for obtaining tenders.
                              ACTION: Mrs. Cash, Mr. Black & Mrs. Drabble

4.    Minutes of the last meeting held 25th March: Members agreed to amend
      item 6, Binbags, to read "Mrs. Cash will contact the Borough Council
      about the shortage of black bags." The minutes were approved as a
      correct record.


5.    Arrangements for the A.G.M. The Secretary reported these are
      proceeding satisfactorily. The Town Hall has been booked for 7th
      July and Councillor Jones has agreed to be the speaker. Catering
      is to be arranged by Mrs. Brewer who asked members for contributions.
                              ACTION: All members


6.    Outing to Southport: The Secretary reported this had been a success
      and over 50 people had taken part.


7.    Purchase of Disco Equipment: Members agreed Mr. Hyman should
      purchase this as soon as possible.
                              ACTION: Mr. Hyman

8.    Treasurer's Report: Mr. Black reported the current account stands
      at £840.57 and the deposit account at £ 991.25


9.    Fund-Raising Committee: Mrs. Drabble reported that a Jumble
      Sale had been organised for the 26th June, 2.30pm at Fulshaw
      House, and a Cheese and Wine Party for the 7th June, 7.30pm,
      also at Fulshaw House, Tickets £2. Members were asked to support
      these events.
                              ACTION: All members

      The meeting closed at 9.15pm. the next meeting will be held on 27th May
```

● There are two aspects to taking minutes:

Taking notes

● take brief, relevant, notes under a heading for each agenda item.

● leave several blank lines between your notes on each item in case members refer back to that point at a later stage in the meeting.

● make a note of what action is decided upon and who is to carry out that action.

● if, at the end of an item, you are unsure about what has been decided, always ask the chairperson to summarise.

● keep your rough notes until after the minutes have been approved at the next meeting: you may need to refer back to them if there is any doubt about what happened.

Writing up the minutes

● prepare a rough draft as soon as possible after the meeting. If you are in any doubt, check with the chairperson or a member.

● your minutes should be brief but accurate. There is no need to record who said what and when. Simply record the decision which was reached and any factors which were of relevance to that decision.

● an 'Action' column on the right hand side of the page is a popular method of highlighting who is responsible for carrying out each decision.

● avoid complicated numbering systems but at the same time do ensure it is possible to refer back to old minutes when necessary.

● keep minutes in a hard-backed ring binder or notebook, together with any reports or papers which were presented to the meeting.

When the chairperson has checked your minutes circulate them to members as soon as possible. Some groups like to send them out within a few days of the meeting so members are reminded of what action they agreed to and have the time to do it before the next meeting. Other groups find it too expensive to send out minutes separately from agendas and instead take good care to get their agendas out with the minutes a week to ten days in advance of the next meeting.

Finally, it is **not** the role of the secretary to lead the meeting. The secretary acts as a prompt to the chairperson, passing him or her the appropriate papers, ensuring that the meeting is adequately prepared and recorded. A good secretary is worth his or her weight in gold, although all too often the holder of this position is undervalued and blamed for anything that goes wrong.

A minutes checklist:

■ keep brief notes in a rough notebook.

■ prepare a rough draft as soon as possible after the meeting.

■ keep minutes brief but accurate.

■ record the decision which was reached and who is responsible for carrying out that decision.

■ keep minutes in a hard-backed folder together with any papers which were presented to the meeting.

▷The role of the chairperson

As the key figure in the organisation, the chairperson's duties will include:

● regular attendance

● planning and preparation, in liaison with the secretary.

● conducting the meeting efficiently and controlling the discussion without monopolising it.

● making sure everyone has the chance to put their views to the meeting.

● making sure the purpose of the meeting is clear and that it is achieved.

- ensuring the meeting keeps to time.
- ensuring the meeting is properly recorded by the secretary.

To perform all these tasks the chairperson will need to know:

- the organisation's aims, activities and methods of working.
- something of the other members' strengths and weaknesses.
- the political and legal environment in which the group operates.

▷ How to chair a meeting

Naturally skilful chairpersons are rare. It is not always the extrovert or natural leader who makes the best chairperson, although some leadership qualities are required. The skills of chairing meetings can be acquired to some extent, however, and depend upon an ability to listen patiently whilst remaining aware of what else is happening around the meeting-table, and not being afraid of making unpopular statements. Here are some guidelines to help you acquire these skills:

Conducting the meeting

- **begin the meeting with a short statement** summarising the purpose of the meeting, what facts are known already, why a decision is required and how you intend to structure the meeting in order to reach a decision.

- **try to separate fact from opinion by** asking members for the facts first. Summarise these and then go on to seek members' opinions.

- **guide the meeting with a summary at each stage** of the discussion so that everyone is clear about what has been achieved so far. At the end of the discussion, summarise the decision which has been reached and who is responsible for implementing that decision.

Guiding the meeting with questions

- **encourage participation by asking leading questions.** It is not the role of the chairperson to spend two hours telling people what they think should be done. Use questions to draw out the quieter members and those with special expertise or to deal with those who monopolise discussions by criticising others.

There are six types of question:

● the **open** question to obtain information "What experience do any of you have in this matter?"

● the **overhead** question addressed to the whole group "What solutions can we suggest?"

● the **relay** question in response to a question "That's an interesting question. How would the rest of you deal with that situation?"

● the **direct** question to individuals, either to draw out special expertise or the quieter members, or to keep the discussion going "I wonder, Mr. X, if you can tell us about your group's work in this area?"

● the **re-directed** question, bringing more people in to the discussion "Mrs. Y, do you feel the suggestions put forward by Mr. X would be relevant to your group's situation?"

● the **reverse** question, asking the person who posed the question to answer it themselves "I understand you had to face this problem once. Perhaps you could tell us how you succeeded in overcoming it?"

How to convey bad news

Questions are a useful way of keeping the discussion flowing without the chairperson having to do all the talking. But there are occasions when the chairperson has to make a substantial personal contribution.

Conveying good news to a meeting is relatively easy. Conveying bad news is difficult as it invariably makes you unpopular. It is essential, however, to let members know bad news to ensure that they feel fully involved in their organisation. You will be far more unpopular if you allow a situation to deteriorate further without trying to call on the goodwill of your colleagues.

Here are some hints on how to convey bad news:

● try to find a positive side and end on a hopeful note.

● state the facts clearly and accurately.

● seek the help of members in finding a remedy.

● it may help to rehearse what you are going to say so you don't lose the thread of what you're trying to tell them, or miss out any essential facts.

Chairpersons also often have to deal with 'difficult' people – the non-stop talker, or the know-alls, or the people who agree to one thing in the meeting and then spend the next month criticising that decision. Here the chairperson has to combine the roles of diplomat and politician. When quieter people make a contribution to the discussion be sure to thank them for it and refer to their point at a later stage of the discussion. Try using the reverse question to quieten the constant critic. Invite other members to question the know-all so he or she gets out of their depth!

Although the chairperson on many occasions has to be firm in their control of the discussion, avoid the temptation of showing any discourtesy or irritation towards members. Not only does this lose the willingness of these difficult members it can also back-fire and cause you to lose the support of useful members, in particular the quieter and less experienced committee members.

■ make sure you have the up-to-date facts on all matters on the agenda.

■ use summaries and questions to guide the meeting.

■ encourage participation but avoid domination by a few members.

■ be prepared to be unpopular at times if it is for the benefit of the organisation.

6 LOOKING AFTER THE MONEY

▷ Why do you need accounts?
▷ How do you prepare a budget?
▷ What is the treasurer's job?
▷ How to open a bank account
▷ How do you keep the accounts?
▷ The benefits of charitable status

▷ Why do you need accounts?

For most people, keeping accounts is a chore. The position of treasurer is often the most unpopular job in any voluntary group. But, whether we like it or not, accounts have to be kept because **you are accountable** to whatever government department or charitable trust has given you the money. They need to know how you have spent it because they, in turn, are accountable to the electorate or the trust's members.

Accounts provide the group with a **valuable source of information** about its activities. They can tell you whether you have overspent or underspent in a particular area of work, or whether you are paying more than you should be for a certain service, and so forth.

In fact, the job of treasurer need not be terribly time-consuming or complicated providing you establish a proper financial system from the start, and then keep it up to date. In this chapter we shall be looking briefly at how to work out a budget for your group and then set up a simple accounts system to manage your money when you receive it. Then we shall go on to look at what tax relief and other benefits are available to charities.

▷ How do you prepare a budget?

Before you can start to apply for funding from your local council or any charitable trusts you have to work out how much money you need, firstly to get the group started and then to continue in business.

Some definitions:

● **capital costs** are the one-off, visible, items of expenditure such as construction of a building, purchase of office equipment, furniture, minibus, slide projector and so on.

● **operating costs** are those expenses which occur again and again, such as heating and lighting bills, stationery, telephone bills, postage and insurance.

If your group is just starting up, it is likely that your capital and operating costs will be far higher in the first year than in subsequent years when you will only need to replace some capital items. Future operating costs will not include, for example, the price of artwork for your stationery.

If you are applying for funding for a number of years ahead, you will need to prepare a budget for each of those years.

Don't make wild guesses. Try to get hold of the costs of several projects similar to yours which have been running for some time and base your estimates on these. Don't exaggerate any items as you will only have to justify why your costs appear to be so far above the norm. Nor is there any point in underestimating your costs in the hope that your application will be more successful.

Generally speaking local authorities, government departments and charitable trusts are more concerned to fund projects whose aims are in line with their own grant-making principles. If they support the aims of the project then they will grant-aid it at whatever cost it takes to ensure its success. If you underestimate you will be unable to carry out the activities you have committed yourself to and your funders will be more critical of you for this than if you had presented a realistic application in the first place.

- make a list of all the items for which you are likely to need money.

- divide these into capital and operating items.

- realistically estimate the cost of each item.

- look ahead – allow for inflation, depreciation, changes in your group's activities, and anything else which might effect your budget.

Overleaf is an example of a typical budget for a community group, covering 3 years. For most applications however, you will only have to set out the first year but it is always a good idea to have a plan for your future activities and the financial effect of these.

EXAMPLE: ANYTOWN COMMUNITY GROUP:
ESTIMATED EXPENDITURE 1984-1986

ITEM	1984		1985[1]		1986[1]	
(see footnotes)	Capital	Operating	Capital	Operating	Capital	Operating
Capital						
(2) Typewriter	200					
(2) Duplicator	200					
(2) Minibus			10,000			
(2) Office Furniture	1,000					
(2) Video Equipment					2,000	
Operating						
(3) Staff salaries (inc.						
employers NI)		10,000		11,000		12,100
Rent		500		550		605
Rates		200		220		242
(7) Heat & Light		1,250		1,375		1,513
(4) Telephone		650		650		715
Postage		400		440		484
(4) Stationery		550		500		550
Publicity & Ads		200		220		242
Staff Recruitment						
(ads)		100		110		121
Insurance		80		88		97
Training Courses		250		275		303
(5) Travel Expenses		500		1,000		1,100
(6) Bank and Audit						
fees		250		275		303
(2) Depreciation:						
Equipment &						
Furniture				150		165
Minibus						1,100
	1,400	14,930	10,000	16,853	2,000	19,640

NOTES

(1) Inflation has been taken into account at the rate of 10% per annum.

(2) These are items which will need to be replaced at some time in the future so each year you will want to put aside some money towards their replacement. In this example, all of these items have been given a 'life' of 10 years and so the amount allowed for their annual depreciation in value is 10% of their current price in the first year following their purchase, plus 10% allowance for inflation in subsequent years. Some funding organisations will not allow you to include depreciation in your budgets and you will need to check this with them beforehand. Alternatively, you can describe 'depreciation of Equipment and Furniture' as 'Replacement of Equipment and Furniture' and replace certain items each year.

(3) When budgeting for staff salaries don't forget to include Employers' N.I. Contributions. For registered charities in April 1983 this was 10.45%, and for others 11.95%.

(4) The allowance for inflation for the telephone has not been applied in 1985 because your costs in 1984 will be higher as you will have to pay the installation charge. The same applies to stationery if you have to pay for the artwork on your headed letters.

(5) These rise steeply in 1985 because you will have the additional expenses of licensing and insuring the minibus.

(6) Auditors' fee are approximately 1% of your annual turnover. Allowance has also been made for bank charges.

(7) Heating and lighting: In your first year, rather than trying to guess the costs of running a building you should try to get hold of the actual costs incurred by a few projects similar to your own and base your estimates on these.

▷What is the treasurer's job?

The treasurer has overall responsibility for the group's finances. This does not mean they have to do everything – you may have a paid member of staff to do the day-to-day book-keeping – but it remains your job to make sure it is done properly. Your tasks will include:

● preparing budgets, and possibly co-ordinating fund-raising efforts.

● handling or overseeing all financial transactions – paying the bills, banking the money, issuing receipts and so on.

● systematically recording these financial transactions.

● reporting to the management committee and the funders about the group's financial position and ensuring the money is spent on the items for which it was given.

● preparing the Annual Accounts which will be passed on to the auditor and then presented to the Annual General Meeting.

▷How to open a bank account

Within a short time of launching your group you will need to open a current bank account. It is usual to authorise up to 4 people as signatories for cheques, although only 2 signatures are normally required, as this covers you for holidays and illnesses. One of the signatories should be the treasurer. The signatories are appointed at a meeting and the bank will require a copy of the minutes of that meeting to be attached to their mandate form. You do not need a separate bank account for each of the group's various activities: your accounts book will show the various headings for which money was received or spent.

An exception is if you receive money from the Manpower Services Commission (MSC) for a temporary employment scheme. You will have to keep all transactions relating to that scheme in a separate account. The MSC also require you to submit monthly claim forms and they will show you how to complete them.

If you receive any large sums of money which you don't require immediately, such as an annual grant paid at the start of the year, you can open a deposit account so you earn interest on it and simply transfer a certain amount each month to your current account.

►How do you keep the accounts?

Your financial transactions will be broken down into 3 types:

● income you receive

● payments by cheque

● petty cash, income and payments

Income you receive

This has to be recorded in a **Cash Received Book**. It should show the date you received the money, the amount, what it was for and whether it was cash or cheque. You should give each transaction a number corresponding to the copy of the receipt slip which you must give to the donor. These copy-receipts should be filed in number order so you can quickly check that all monies received were entered in the **Cash Received Book** and then banked. Receipts made out in error and cancelled must also be kept, so that every number is accounted for. Standard receipt books are available from most stationery shops.

In the **Cash Received Book** you should make a note of when you banked the money so this too can be checked against the monthly bank statement. At the end of each month you should total the columns, check out any discrepancies and start a new page for the following month.

				ANALYSIS COLUMNS						
				Grants		Income from school	Subs & donations	Income from events	Sundry income	BANK
Date	Details	Ref	Total	Once off	Revenue					
1982										
April 1	LBH – grant	1	5,500	2,000	3,500					
2	Income – school	2	125			125				5,625
23	Subs & donations	3	50				50			
28	Jumble sale	4	125					125		175
			5,800	2,000	3,500	125	50	125		5,800

CASH RECEIVED ANALYSIS BOOK

Payments by cheque

The transactions are recorded in a **Cash Paid Book** which shows the date of each payment, to whom it was paid, the cheque number and the total amount. You should also have columns for each heading of your budgeted expenditure and put the amount into the appropriate column so that when you total the columns at the end of the month you can see exactly how much you spent on each item. This will help you prepare monthly and annual statements, when all you have to do is add up the monthly totals for each item. Keep any cancelled cheque stubs as well as used stubs. Once a week or month you will need to draw out some petty cash by cheque. This should also be recorded in the **Cash Paid** book.

All in £ — CASH PAID ANALYSIS BOOK

Date	Details	Reference Cheque No	Total	Furniture & equipment	Salaries & N.I.	Admin expenses	Rents, rates, light & heat	Travel	Insurance	Audit	Training & conferences	Mother-tongue classes	Petty cash	Sundry expenses & events
1982														
April 2	Petty cash	250	50										50	
5	GLC	251	2,000	2,000										
7	Trojan – printing	252	60			60								
	Stacey Ltd – stationery	253	40			40								
	LBH – rent, rates, light & heat	254	300				300							
8	Co-op	255	100						100					
10	GLC	256	20								20			
28	Hasibe Ali	257	490		490									
30	Inland Revenue	258	290		290									
	A.N. Other – cleaning	259	20											20
	Workers Electric Ltd	260	25											25
	Petty cash	261	45										45	
			3,440	2,000	780	100	300	—	100	—	20	—	95	45

* Administration expenses include stationery, post, photocopying, telephone, advertising.

Comparing your accounts books with the bank statements

Once a month you will need to reconcile the accounts books with the bank statements which you should have sent to you at the end of each month. Because it takes several days for a cheque to go through the banking system, you will find some items are not shown on the bank statement. On the other hand, the statement will show some items which are not included in your accounts books, such as bank charges or interest on any overdraft. These should be entered in your book before attempting the reconciliation.

By comparing the two, you can draw up a **Monthly Reconciliation Account** on which you can base your report to the Management Committee.

Total of Cash Received Analysis Book on 30 April 1982	£5,800
Less: Total of Cash Paid Analysis Book on 30 April 1982	3,440
	£2,360

The way we reconcile these two figures is worked out like this:

Balance as per bank statement dated 30 April 1982				£2,255
Less: **Uncleared cheques**				
Date	**Name**	**Chq. no.**	**£**	
April 30	Workers Electric	260	25	
	Petty cash	261	45	70
				£2,185
Add: **Deposits not shown on statement**				
Date				
April 28	(Jumble sale & donation)			175
				£2,360

Petty cash

A Petty Cash Book (overleaf) shows when you took that cash out of the bank and when and how you spent it. Always get a receipt for every item of expenditure met from your petty cash. You should also write out a **Petty Cash Voucher,** explaining what the cash was used for, and file it with the receipt attached, in numerical order. If it is not possible to get a receipt – perhaps it was paid to an individual volunteer as re-imbursement for bus fares – then the person receiving the cash should sign the voucher.

PETTY CASH ANALYSIS BOOK

Income			Expenditure						
Date	Details	Total	Date	Details	Ref.	Total	Admin expenses	Travel	Sundry
1982 April 2	Cash from bank	50	1982 April 6	Hasibe – fares	1	3		3	
			7	Coffee & milk	2	4	4		
			14	Hasibe – fares	3	6		6	
			21	Hasibe – fares	4	5		5	
			28	Jumble sale	5	20			20
30	Cash from bank	45	30	Hasibe – fares	6	7		7	
		95		Total expenditure		45		21	24
				Cash in hand not yet spent		50			
						95			

HACKNEY ETHNIC MINORITIES ASSOCIATION
Income and Expenditure Account and Budget Comparison for the month of April 1982

	One month's Actual		One month's budget
	£	£	£
Income			
Grant: LBH – once off	2,000		
– 1 month	1,167	3,167	3,167
Income from school fees		125	–
Income from subs & donations		50	–
Income from events		125	–
		3,467	3,167
Less **Expenditure**			
Furniture & equipment	2,000		2,000
Salaries and N.I.	780		781
Administration expenses	100		83
Rent, rates, light & heat	100		100
Travel	21		33
Insurance	8		8
Audit	–		9
Training & conferences	20		16
Mother tongue teaching	100		83
Sundry – events	69		54
Total expenditure		3,198	3,167
Excess of Income over Expenditure		269	NIL

Preparation of an Income and Expenditure Account

Once a month, or each quarter year, you will want to give the Management Committee a full statement of the group's financial position showing how much has been spent to date, and on what. You may also want to compare this with the budget so the Management Committee can see whether they are on target with their spending, or may be left with insufficient money to cover the last two or three months of the year. This means that your budget figures for the year will have to be divided by 12 for a monthly statement or 4 for a quarterly statement.

Any income you receive to cover a period longer than that covered in your statement will have to be apportioned similarly: an annual grant from your local authority will have to be divided by 12 or 4. See opposite.

Annual Accounts

At the end of each year you have to produce two financial statements:

● **An Annual Income and Expenditure Account.** This is an accumulation of your monthly/quarterly statements.

● **A Balance Sheet.** This shows the financial position of an organisation at the end of the financial year. But unlike the Income and Expenditure Accounts it also shows your assets - - what the group owns and advance payments at that point in time against your liabilities – what you owe at that point in time. Besides working out the cash aspects of the Balance Sheet such as cash at bank, petty cash in hand, you will need also to do stock checks on such items as stationery, equipment, furniture, food stocks and so on. These items have to be valued at cost, less depreciation, where applicable. See overleaf.

Auditing the accounts

Community groups who are registered limited companies must, by law, have their accounts audited by a qualified practising auditor. Other groups which are not limited companies may prefer to use an independent, but financially knowledgeable, person as their auditor.

HACKNEY ETHNIC MINORITIES ASSOCIATION
Balance Sheet at 30 April 1982

	£	£
Fixed Assets		nil
Current Assets		
Cash at bank	2,360	
Cash in hand (petty cash)	50	
Prepayments: rent, rates, etc.	200	
insurance	92	2,702
Less: Current Liabilities		
LBH grant paid in advance	2,333	
Mother tongue teaching	100	(2,433)
		269
This is made up of:		nil
Accumulated fund 1.4.82		
Surplus of Income over Expenditure		
for April 1982	269	269

Handwritten annotations:

- This is the difference between the Cash Received and Cash Paid Analysis Books
- This is the unspent money in the Petty Cash box
- These are the items of expenditure outside the period (see Expenditure Working Sheet, page 12)
- This is the amount of grant outside the period (see Income Working Sheet, page 11)
- This is an item of expenditure incurred in the period but not paid at 30 April called Accrual (see Expenditure Working Sheet)
- This is the excess of Income over Expenditure (see Income and Expenditure Account, page 13)

72

An audit is simply an independent confirmation that the funds were spent in the way stated in the annual accounts. The auditor will want to see all your accounts books, files of petty cash vouchers and copy-receipts, your bank statements and cheque stubs. They will also want to see an up-to-date list of all items of value owned by the group, such as stationery left in stock, and may carry out a random check on these. Minutes of Committee meetings will also be examined to ensure you spent the money in accordance with the Committee's instructions.

If the auditor is satisfied with the way the group has managed its financial affairs they will issue a statement which should be attached to the printed annual accounts, saying they have examined the group's accounts and are satisfied that they give a true picture of the organisation's financial position.

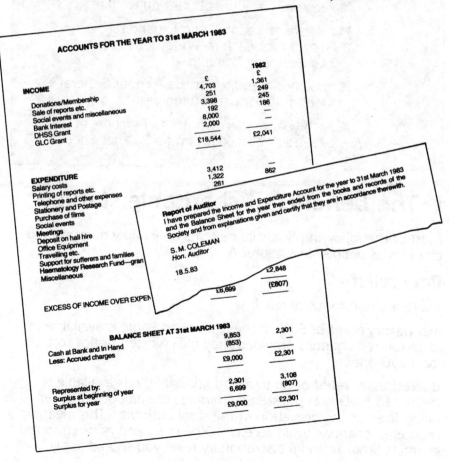

ACCOUNTS FOR THE YEAR TO 31st MARCH 1983

		1982
	£	£
INCOME	4,703	1,361
Donations/Membership	251	249
Sale of reports etc.	3,398	245
Social events and miscellaneous	192	186
Bank Interest	8,000	—
DHSS Grant	2,000	—
GLC Grant		
	£18,544	£2,041

EXPENDITURE		
Salary costs	3,412	—
Printing of reports etc.	1,322	862
Telephone and other expenses	261	
Stationery and Postage		
Purchase of films		
Social events		
Meetings		
Deposit on hall hire		
Office Equipment		
Travelling etc.		
Support for sufferers and families		
Haematology Research Fund—gran...		
Miscellaneous		
		£2,848
EXCESS OF INCOME OVER EXPEN...	16,699	(£807)

Report of Auditor
I have prepared the Income and Expenditure Account for the year to 31st March 1983 and the Balance Sheet for the year then ended from the books and records of the Society and from explanations given and certify that they are in accordance therewith.

S. M. COLEMAN
Hon. Auditor

18.5.83

BALANCE SHEET AT 31st MARCH 1983

Cash at Bank and in Hand	9,853	2,301
Less: Accrued charges	(853)	—
	£9,000	£2,301
Represented by:	2,301	3,108
Surplus at beginning of year	6,699	(807)
Surplus for year		
	£9,000	£2,301

■ have you got enough cheque signatories to cover holidays and sickness?

■ arrange to have a bank statement sent to you each month.

■ put into a deposit account any large sums of money you receive early.

■ have you got:
a Cash Received Book
a Cash Paid Book
a Petty Cash Book
a stock of petty cash and receipts vouchers?

■ keep your accounts books up to date

■ prepare an Income and Expenditure Account for each meeting of the Management Committee.

■ appoint an auditor at the Annual General Meeting for the following year.

■ each year prepare an Annual Income and Expenditure Account and a Balance Sheet.

▷ The benefits of charitable status

Most of the following financial benefits only apply to registered charities as defined in Chapter 4.

Rate relief

There are two forms of relief:

mandatory relief of 50% of the rates chargeable is available to all registered charities provided they give written notice to the local authority.

discretionary relief of up to an additional 50% is available to registered AND non-registered charities, the amount of relief being fixed at the discretion of the local authority. This means registered charities could receive 100% relief and non-registered charities 50%. To claim discretionary relief you should apply in writing to your local authority as soon as your group looks like acquiring premises as it cannot be granted restrospectively.

Both types of rate relief depend upon the premises being used wholly or mainly for charitable purposes. The group claiming the relief must be the occupant and not just the owner of the premises.

Under the 1976 Rating (Charity Shops) Act, relief is also given to charities occupying a shop wholly or mainly for the sale of goods donated to the charity provided all proceeds of the sale, after deduction of expenses, are used for charitable purposes.

Some groups may be exempt from payment of rates depending on what they use the premises for. For non-registered charities unable to get more than 50% discretionary relief it may be better to apply to the local authority for this exemption on the basis of what the building is used for, rather than on the basis of their charitable or community system.

Some local authorities encourage community groups to apply under this arrangement for exemption as these are then refunded to the local authority by central government whereas the discretionary rate relief has to be met by the local authority.

The three main categories for rates exemption are:

● **unoccupied buildings** – if you own or rent a building but are not using it yet you will not have to pay rates on the property.

● **places of religious worship** – this applies only to places of worship belonging to the established churches.

● **institutions for the disabled** – this exemption is available to organisations providing residential accommodation, workshop and training facilities, and other welfare services for the disabled.

Gifts to charity

These benefits to registered charities fall into four categories:

● **covenants**

● **gifts of capital**

● **gifts in kind**

● **sponsorship**

Covenants

Many charities fail to take advantage of the tax benefits offered on covenanted donations either because they fear it is very complicated or because their organisations are unlikely to attract such donations anyway. Of the four groups referred to at the start of this book only one, Feltham Community Association, actually goes out to collect donations by covenant.

A Deed of Covenant is a simple legal agreement by a donor, whether an individual or a company, to make regular payments to a beneficiary. The charity is able to recover the tax that has been paid on the amount specified in the covenant. For example, if a donor agrees to pay £100 out of his or her taxed income each year to the 'ABC Charity' they will be able to claim back £30 (assuming 30% base rate of tax) and so the donation is worth £130. The same applies to companies which give to charities under a deed of covenant: they are able to offset the cash gift against their liability to corporation tax.

Alternatively, the donor may permit the charity to reclaim the tax thereby increasing the value of the donation. Covenants have to last for a minimum of four years, but the tax is reclaimed annually and the charity must be registered. In Northern Ireland and Scotland where there is no registration process the Inland Revenue will determine whether the organisation is charitable – see Chapter 4. The aim of this tax relief is to encourage charitable giving.

Gifts of capital

Gifts made during the donor's lifetime to registered UK charities are exempt from capital transfer tax providing they are made more than one year before the donor's death. If the donor dies less than a year after the gift is made, or if they make a legacy or bequest to a UK charity, there will be exemption on the first £250,000 of such gifts.

It is possible, however, to extend the advantages of the covenant method by making out a loan covenant. Under this method the donor agrees to a loan of a sum of money to a registered charity and for the repayments to be made out of the amount they save in taxation. The loan covenant can include a clause to waive repayment of the loan on the death of the donor which means the question of capital transfer tax is avoided altogether.

Covenants may sound complicated but they are nothing more than a simple form which you can either draw up yourself – see page 80 – or arrange through a solicitor. Once the forms have been drawn up and approved by the Inland Revenue it is very straightforward to operate and the Inland Revenue will advise you on how to reclaim the tax.

Covenants are a good way of increasing your funds as membership subscriptions can also be paid in this way.

Gifts in kind

Gifts in kind, such as a building, made to a charity exempt the donor from paying capital gains tax on the disposal of these assets. Also the charity is exempt from paying capital gains tax if it later sells those assets, such as a building.

Sponsorship

Besides saving corporation tax by giving to charity under deeds of covenant, companies can undertake sponsorship of the activities of one or more charities. Sponsorship may be no more than a publicised donation or a limited form of advertising. It can, however, extend to company involvement in the sponsored project through time, effort and personnel, and could even be directly linked to marketing policy. Charities applying to companies for sponsorship should therefore phrase their applications in such a way as to point out any relevant commercial benefits to the company. Obtaining advertisements from companies for annual reports and other publications is a simple and popular form of sponsorship.

Investment of charity funds

Charities are exempt from tax on most forms of investment income, providing the income is used for charitable purposes. Forms of investment income include interest and dividends, rent and other profits from property belong to the charity. Charities can take advantage of this by negotiating for the whole of their annual grant to be paid in advance and ensuring that all grants are received on time and then invested until required in a building society or bank deposit account. One way of easing administration of this money and ensuring maximum interest is obtained is to use the services of the Official Custodian for Charities at 57-60 Haymarket, London SW1Y 4QZ. The Official Custodian also provides a service for the management of charities' property investment which carry relief from income tax and capital gains tax as well as exemption from stamp duty and development land tax.

Charitable trading

A registered charity cannot be established for the sole purpose of trade but trading may be carried on if it is in pursuit of the charity's charitable purposes as set out in Chapter 4. In other words trading is permitted only as a means, not an end. The profits from this trading are only exempt from taxation if they are used for the charitable purposes of the organisation. Profits made on goods which were donated to the organisation are not taxable. A charity shop selling only donated items will have no tax liability on its profits.

Value Added Tax and joint purchasing

In general charities are not able to reclaim VAT because the money they receive is not considered to have come their way as a result of a business activity. In order to assist community groups with this problem, some local authorities have agreed to purchase items like stationery and office equipment, on behalf of community groups and then to give these items back to the community group after making the appropriate deduction from their grant. The Greater London Council acts as a purchasing consortium for community groups operating within Greater London. It is well worth approaching your local authority to see if they have such a service and if not whether they would consider starting one.

Providing that a retiring Auditor shall not be automatically re-appointed by virtue of this rule if notice of an intended resolution to appoint another person in his/her place has been given in accordance with paragraph (e) of this rule and the resolution cannot be proceeded with because of the death, incapacity or ineligibility of that other person.

e) A resolution at a general meeting of the club (i) appointing another person as Auditor in place of a retiring Auditor or (ii) providing expressly that a retiring Auditor shall not be re-appointed shall not be effective unless notice of the intention to move it has been given to the club not less than 28 days before the meeting at which it is moved. On receipt by the club of notice of the intention to move any such resolution the club shall give notice of the resolution to the members and to the retiring Auditor in accordance with Section 6 of the Friendly and Industrial Provident Societies Act 1968, and shall give notice to the members in accordance with that section of any representation made or intended to be made by the retiring Auditor.

f) None of the following persons shall be appointed as Auditor of the club: –
(i) An officer or Servant of the club.
(ii) A person who is a partner of or in the employment of or who employs an officer or Servant of the club or
(iii) A body corporate.

g) The Auditor shall in accordance with section 9 of the Friendly and Industrial and Provident Societies Act 1968 make a report to the club on the accounts examined by him/her and on the revenue account or accounts and the balance sheet of the club for the year of account in respect of which s/he is appointed.

h) The Auditor shall have a right of access at all times to the books, deeds and accounts of the club and to all other documents relating to its affairs, and shall be entitled to require from the officers of the club such information and explanations as s/he thinks necessary for the performance of the duties of the Auditors.

26. NOMINATIONS AND PROCEEDINGS ON DEATH OR BANKRUPTCY

Upon a claim being made by the personal representative of a deceased member or the trustee in bankruptcy of a bankrupt member to any property in the club belonging to the deceased or bankrupt member the club shall transfer or pay such property to which the personal representative or trustee in bankruptcy has become entitled as the personal representative or trustee in bankruptcy may direct them.

A member may in accordance with the Industrial and Provident

16

APPENDIX 4

GROSS DEED OF COVENANT (VARIABLE)

(Recommended for use where a charity establishes a separate trading company)

DEED OF COVENANT

We ....

of ....

hereinafter called **the Company** hereby covenant

with ....

hereinafter called **the charity**.

Whereas the charity is established for charitable purposes only and the Company has decided to make a covenanted donation to charity within the meaning of Section 248 of the Income and Corporation Taxes Act 1970 and to execute and carry out this covenant accordingly.

Now this Deed witnesses as follows:

1. In each accounting period for the purposes of Corporation Tax the Company shall pay to the charity in accordance with the provisions of this Deed an annual sum equal to the income of the Company of that period the sum to be paid less income tax, and for the purposes of this Deed 'the income of the company' shall mean its distributable profits as defined in paragraph 10 of Schedule 16 of the Finance Act 1972 but without deducting:

   (a) the amount of Corporation Tax which but for the said Section 248 would be payable in respect thereof, or

   (b) the annual sum payable under these presents.

2. The covenant hereinbefore contained shall commence within and include the accounting period during which the same is executed and shall continue until and including the accounting period ending on or after the

   .... day of ....

3. Payments herein should be made annually in such manner and at such times as the company thinks fit and subject thereto the company shall at least 21 days before the end of each accounting period pay (less income tax) a sum equal to the income of the company of that period as then estimated and in the event of any overpayment the excess shall be refunded at or after the end of the said period and in the event of any underpayment the shortfall shall be made good (less income tax) before the end of the said period.

7 GETTING THE MONEY

▷ **How do you apply for a grant?**
▷ **Government grants**
▷ **What are charitable trusts?**
▷ **Raising money from industry**

DON'T TELL ME — YOU'RE OFF TO COLLECT OUR GRANT, RIGHT?

▶How do you apply for a grant?

Preparing your application

Whether you are applying to the public or private sector, and whether you want cash or services in kind, the rules for writing an application are pretty much the same.

Presentation

● always address your letter of application to a named person. If you don't know who to write to, phone up and ask for the name and job title of the appropriate person.

● your letter should be no longer than two sides of A4 paper. If necessary, attach to this no more than a further two sheets of paper setting out your budget and any other vital information, such as an eye-catching leaflet.

● all letters should be neatly and individually typed – untidy duplicated letters are destined for the bin. If you need to type hundreds of applications then it is worth getting the job done on a word processor at your local Information Technology Centre (see Chapter 11) or a commercial secretarial agency.

Content

Make your letter sound positive and enthusiastic – talk about your successes, not your failures; and your hopes for the future, not your fears. But always be realistic: there's no point in promising them you can achieve the earth for only £100 when you know that's impossible.

Your letter should cover the following points:

● **introduction** – who you are and the aims of your organisation.

● **a summary of the problem you intend to tackle.** Try to define it as closely as possible, supporting your case with a few hard facts – such as the higher than average percentage of elderly people in your neighbourhood, and the increasing scale of their problems. Use emotive phrases but don't overdo the lurid detail!

● **state the objectives of your project and the methods you**

will use in overcoming the outlined problem. You may want to refer to the achievements of other groups which have employed similar methods, or refer to the shortcomings of other methods and explain how yours differ from these.

● **state the amount you require from them.** Refer the reader to the detailed budget. This should set out all your expenses, similar to the example on page 64 in the last chapter. Presenting the whole of your budget prevents the potential funder from blithely lopping off a round 10% or 20% as he or she should be able to see that the project is not viable without all of the ingredients; you can't do without insurance or electricity. This is why it is vital for you to prepare a realistic budget as accurately as possible.

● **say how you intend to evaluate your work.** We will be looking at evaluation in Chapter 11 but a statement of intent to monitor your own work suggests a responsibility and determination to meet your own objectives.

● if possible, say **how you intend the project should be funded in the future** – whether it will be able to continue on the income it will generate for itself, or whether your local authority has promised support at a later date. You can also mention at this stage any commitment or support you have received from elsewhere, e.g. the local Trades Council, other community groups etc.

Who to apply to

Just as there is no point in applying for a job as a typist when you can't type, so there is no point in applying to the Arts Council for a grant to build a Sports Hall. Choose which government department, trusts or firms are likely to consider projects of your type and concentrate your efforts on those few. For government departments there are a number of books which list their criteria for making grants (listed in Chapter 12, 'Resources'), and the Directory of Grant-Making Trusts lists information about all the charitable trusts in the United Kingdom.

It is well worth doing this research. It may save you hours of typing, time which can more usefully be put to following up a few well-chosen potential funders. Look through other groups'

Annual Reports and see where they got their money from and try to get the name of a person to write to.

Follow-up

A week or so after you've sent off your application, you can begin your lobbying. Perhaps you've included at the end of your application letter a suggestion that they contact you about a visit to your centre or a meeting to discuss your group's work in more detail. Exactly how and who you lobby is a matter of judgement and depends upon your particular circumstances. It is worth trying to find out the 'hidden' power structure within the government department, or local council, to which you've applied. For example, is the chairperson of the relevant committee popular within his or her own group of councillors – is he or she a part of the caucus? To what extent does he or she get involved in decisions about what should go before full committee, or does he or she rely upon his or her chief officer's views?

At national level where civil servants are dealing with hundreds of grant applications a phone call from you will at least get your letter back to the top of the pile in the pending tray. Again, a question in Parliament by your MP about the work of organisations such as yours – be sure to get your name mentioned – will restore it to the top of the pile. Don't be afraid of appearing persistent – but always politely of course! It shows your determination and commitment to your project. It is all too easy to be put off and become downhearted when you get a few rejections; as with job applications you will be rejected many times over and the only thing you can do is to go on trying. If your project is sound and credible you'll get there in the end.

And after you've got your grant

When you've got your grant cheque in your hand, don't forget to straightaway write to the donor/minister/civil servant/local government officer/local council chairperson/managing director/ trust secretary to thank them, and promise to keep them informed of your activities. And then don't forget to do that! Send them a copy of your newsletter or annual report, with their name included in the list of donors, or an invitation to your open day. All of these things help to keep you in their mind and ease the way for your application the following year.

- always send your application to a named person.
- keep your letter short and to the point and have it neatly typed.
- always sound positive – but realistic.
- carefully select the organisations you apply to.
- be persistent but polite in following up applications.
- always thank the donor and keep in touch with them.

▷ Government grants

The first thing you need to decide is what level of government you should approach for a grant.
   You have a choice of five levels:

- headquarters of central government departments
- local government – district and county councils
- regional authorities ● Quangos ● EEC

The five stories at the start of this book show the ways you can combine grants and income from different sources:

Sickle Cell Society Manpower Services Commission, Dept. of Health & Social Security, Greater London Council, trusts' fund-raising event, companies and individuals.

Feltham Community Association Trading (their bar and co-operative resources centre), one grant from the local Council, one grant from a trust, local companies and individuals, fund-raising events.

Macclesfield Womens' Aid Manpower Services Commission, District and County Council, fund-raising events, local companies and individuals, DHSS (rent payments for women stayinc at the Refuge).

Earlstown Opportunity Group Urban programme (District Council and Dept. of Environment), fund-raising events, local companies and individuals.

Sunnyside Gardens Brighter Islington Campaign, the GLC, Urban Aid, Shell Better Britain Campaign, the Allen Lane/British Trust for Conservation Volunteers Tree Planting Campaign, fund-raising events.

Central government grants

Central government departments tend to fund only national organisations, or those with national significance, such as a pilot or experimental project which, if successful, may be extended nationally. Also central government departments will only fund those voluntary organisations whose aims fall within their particular area of responsibility.

There are many occasions where the levels of government overlap, however. At central government level there is the **Voluntary Services Unit.** This is based at the Home Office and assists with applications which do not fall into the remit of any one department. The VSU will contact the various departments involved and help to sort out which department should take the main responsibility. It also has funds of its own to allocate to pilot projects.

Central government support to voluntary organisations falls into three categories:

● where a voluntary service is preferable to a statutory service, usually on financial grounds.

● where voluntary services can usefully complement or supplement statutory services.

● where a voluntary service provides an alternative, or choice, for the consumer.

Here is a list of the main departments which have funds for voluntary organisations (addresses are given in Chapter 12, 'Resources').

● Department of Education and Science – for provision of educational research and services, adult education and voluntary youth organisations.

● Department of Employment – for sheltered employment schemes for disabled people; MSC schemes for temporary employment; other facilities for training for employment.

● Department of Environment – for urban conservation and upkeep of historic buildings; the Urban, Partnership and Inner City Programmes for urban areas of special social need; for road safety; for research and education in planning and design; homelessness and housing advice services.

● Department of Health and Social Security – for childrens'

homes; for voluntary reception and re-establishment centres; help to cover the cost of sending staff working in voluntary organisations on social work training courses; the Opportunities for Volunteering Scheme which aims to increase opportunities for unemployed people to do voluntary work in health and social services; joint finance with health authorities to encourage community care.

● Home Office – for probation hostels; rehabilitation of criminal offenders; research into causes of delinquency and treatment of offenders; the Voluntary Services Unit.

Note: Most government grants are for one year, from April to April. Applications usually need to be sent in five or six months beforehand.

Local government grants

Groups of a local nature have two options – their county council or district council – and choice will depend upon how services are organised in your locality. Metropolitan districts have responsibility for social services and education; in non-metropolitan districts these come under the remit of the county council (see page 192 for duties of local authorities).

Many county and district councils have grants committees. These look at all local applications for grant-aid rather than strictly adhering to departmental responsibilities. Grants made under the Urban Aid scheme and the Partnership and Inner City programmes are made up of 75% central government money and 25% from the local authority, but all applications have to be approved first by the local authority which then submits them to the Department of Environment in an order of priority.

Local government is empowered to make grants to local organisations under numerous Acts of Parliament. The main types of grant aid are for:

● residential care and promotion of the welfare of children

● social and physical recreation for young people

● residential care and promotion of welfare of elderly and disabled people

● homelessness

● information services

● community transport schemes

Each of our five sample groups directly or indirectly fall into several of these categories, for example, Macclesfield Women's Aid provides accommodation for homeless women, an advice service to them, and promotes the welfare of their children.

Besides giving cash grants, local authorities are also empowered to assist community groups with furniture, equipment, vehicles, premises and bulk purchase of goods, which can save you paying VAT.

Much local voluntary activity is funded by local authorities under **Section 137** of the **1972 Local Government Act**. This enables them to spend up to the value of a 2p rate each year on voluntary activities. Some local authorities are more generous than others in their use of this power. If organisations in your district get very little help from the couuncil it is worth finding out how much they spend under this section. If they are not using this power, why not?

Although most of the money for the Urban Programme comes from central government, organisations applying for it first have to obtain the approval of their local council, which prioritises applications and forwards the top few to the Department of Environment. In theory, the local authority makes a commitment to take on the whole financial burden for each project it recommends when the three years of Urban Programme money expires; in practice, cuts in local authority expenditure have meant that a large part of Urban Programme money is spent on maintaining projects set up in the early days of the scheme because the local authorities have been unable to meet their commitment.

Local authority grants are vulnerable to party politics and this may be an important factor when deciding whether to approach your county or district council. If you're in an area which swings from left to right and back again, you will have to tread warily to avoid losing your grant when there is a change in power.

An increasing number of voluntary organisations are negotiating contracts with their local authorities to give themselves greater security. Under these contractual arrangements, the voluntary group agrees to provide a certain service on behalf of the local authority in return for a grant paid as a fee for those services. The most obvious example of a contractual service is where a voluntary organisation provides the local authority with X number of places in a probation hostel or childrens' home and charges the local authority for these places. Recently this idea has been extended, however, to groups running youth centres, information services and others providing a less tangible service to the community.

Regional authorities

In addition there are certain regional structures, most importantly Regional Health Authorities, which cut across county boundaries. The Manpower Services Commission also has regional offices which administer the Youth Training Scheme, the Community Programme, Community Industry, the Voluntary Projects Programme, and sheltered employment and training schemes for the disabled.

Quasi-Autonomous Non-Governmental Organisations (Quangos)

Central Government also funds voluntary organisations through several quangos. These include the Commission for Racial Equality, the Development Commission, the Equal Opportunities Commission, and the Housing Corporation. Addresses of these and the other main grant-aiding quangos are on page 191.

EEC money

European Social Fund

This is the main source of EEC funding for voluntary organisations. The aim of the fund is to improve the employment opportunities for workers in the Common Market and so raise the standard of living.

At the moment (1984) the priority is to help unemployed people under 25 years, the long-term unemployed, women wishing to go back to work, the disabled, migrant workers, and those in small firms. The EEC is particularly keen to encourage innovatory employment projects.

Social fund money is only to cover running costs – capital costs are not met. Nor must the Social Fund grant exceed 50% of the project's total expenditure, so the remainder will have to be raised from another source.

Application forms and further information are available from Department of Employment, Overseas Division (OB2), Caxton House, Tothill Street, London SW1H 9NA (Tel 01-213 4305).

Other Sources of EEC money

These include grants for research into European integration, information and education about the EEC, aid to coal and steel regions, aid for research and development for special housing for handicapped people and migrant workers, human rights, and support of organisations which represent migrant workers.

▷What are charitable trusts?

The Americans use the term 'foundation' to describe what we call charitable trusts which are non-profit making, non-governmental, organisations established for charitable purposes. They have their own capital fund and are managed by wholly independent trustees.

   You should prepare your applications to charitable trusts on the same lines as those outlined at the beginning of this chapter. Here are a few additional points to note about trusts:

Types of charitable trusts

There are two main types:

● independent trusts – many of these were founded by families and individuals around the turn of the century, such as the Joseph Rowntree Memorial Trust

● company trusts – some companies prefer to organise their charitable giving through a trust in order to obtain the tax advantages. The trustees are often directors of the company and may either work independently of shareholders, making their own decisions about which charities to support, or they work much more closely with the company taking into account its marketing and public relations' policies.

Where to find out about trusts

The standard reference book is the **Directory of Grant-Making Trusts**. This classifies all registered charities in England and Wales alphabetically, and also by purpose and locality. It does not, however, include information on trusts with funds available for an area smaller than a district council, or those trusts which have an income of less than £1000 per year. For these you will have to look at the Register of Charities which is maintained by the Charity Commissioners.

A copy of the Register of Charities for northern trusts is kept at Liverpool, and in London for the south. No register is available for charities in Scotland and Northern Ireland as there is no registration process in these places.

The Register and the Directory give details of the kinds of projects which the trusts support and the average size of grant given by each trust.

Timescale

Some trusts only meet once a year to consider applications; others meet at six-monthly or quarterly intervals. You should try to find out the timescale of the trusts you approach and state in your application when you will require the money.

What amount?

The Directory gives the average amount of money each registered trust donates to organisations. There is no point in applying for £10,000 from a trust which only has an income of £5,000 a year and sets a maximum of £1,000 for each project. Pitch your applications at the right level for each trust.

If your project covers a wide range of community activity, it may be better to split it into several packages and apply to the appropriate charitable trusts for the various packages. For example, if you want to open a community centre which will provide a day centre for elderly people as well as an adventure playground, work out your costs for each and send separate applications for each activity to trusts interested in those types of projects. You should, of course, state that they are part of a larger scheme and briefly outline this to show how the smaller part fits into the whole.

Trusts are human!

The trusts' members may want to talk to you or visit your premises before granting you the money. They may have some ideas for developing your project further, or they may ask if you are aware of similar schemes around the country. The larger trusts are managed by full-time professional staff and they want to ensure that the schemes they support will be managed with a similar professional approach, so make sure you know your stuff! And afterwards – as usual, don't forget to send them a thank-you letter, an annual report, and an invitation to the opening day!

▷Raising money from industry

The overall sum given by industry each year is over £50 million and, although this is small compared to the financial support given by charitable trusts and government, it plays a vital part in the development of the voluntary sector. Several very enterprising voluntary projects owe their existence to the support of industry who have not only provided cash but also equipment and staff. So it is worth trying your luck!

A couple of characteristics about company-giving: firstly, companies tend to give lots of small one-off cash grants to spread their goodwill as far as possible; secondly, they generally favour the more conservative sort of voluntary projects about which there is likely to be less risk of controversy.

Some points to bear in mind when making an appeal to industry:

Who to approach

As with charitable trusts it is worth doing a little homework to find out which companies are likely to give to your sort of project. Also, your application is more likely to be well received if you find out the name and title of the person who deals with grant applications. If possible, try to make personal contact with them.

Local groups should approach local firms, including branches of national companies. These often have their own charity budgets. The head offices of large companies usually give donations to national, not local, organisations unless they are in the vicinity of the head office.

A useful book to consult about companies is the CBI's **Kompass Register of British Industry and Companies** which categorises companies by region. Other helpful books are the **Guide to Key British Enterprises** and the **Stock Exchange Official Year Book**, both of which are available from most libraries. The CBI also has lists of members categorised by their products and services. And don't forget the Yellow Pages!

Use your contacts

Never be afraid to use your contacts and those of other members of the group. If you haven't got a contact in a particular firm you want to approach, get in touch with the

Mayor of the local Council or Industrial Development Officer and see if they can help you with one.

If they aren't able to get you a personal introduction they should be able to give you the names of people to contact. Then it's up to you to phone up and say something like "Councillor X suggested I contact you as he thought you would be able to give us some advice." Flattery can get you everywhere! But don't immediately plunge into the question of how much you think they should give you. Explain what your project is about and how you would appreciate their advice with your current financial predicament. It's all a matter of playing it by ear.

As with radio and television interviews, you have to work out whether or not approaching industrialists is a job for which you are suitable. If you feel that your approach lacks enthusiasm and confidence, choose a member who feels comfortable and capable in this type of situation.

If you are not able to make personal contact, don't worry too much. Concentrate your efforts on writing a good letter of application on the lines set out at the beginning of this chapter.

How much should you ask for?

If you've done your homework you'll know whether the company gives small or large, regular or one-off donations. Gear your application accordingly. Some companies prefer to give services in kind, such as printing, furniture, or to second staff. So be precise about what you want and assure them recognition will be given to their generosity. Company donation through sponsorship, secondments, gifts in kind and advertising may be more valuable than a cash donation – and may be more in keeping with the company's policy.

Sponsorship

This is the most visible form of company giving. Sponsorship is when a company agrees to provide financial support to a venture which the charity wants to organise and will associate the company's name with the event.

As with the other forms of fund-raising, you need to do your homework and look at what you can offer to local firms. For example, if you are wanting money to set up an adventure playground, you could approach a local childrens' clothes shop about sponsoring a children's painting competition. They may provide the prizes, the judges, the venue and so on – and you can sell the paintings!

Of course, you have to choose your sponsors with care – you would not want to be associated with any disreputable firms, or those whose products are harmful in some way.

And please don't forget the thanks afterwards!

■ decide what level/s of government to approach and send your application in good time.

■ select charitable trusts according to their criteria for projects, the amount they are able to give, and their timescale.

■ select companies with some connection to your project and check whether they prefer to give donations or sponsorship.

Raising funds - on video

Running a Social and Fund-raising Organisation. That's the title of a new 60 minute video made by the Ford Motor Company. Ford have given NFCO copies in both VHS and Betamax formats and they are available for loan to NFCO members. Write to NFCO if you want to arrange a showing. The video covers organisation, accounts, legal questions and features a look at fundraising by NFCO's Director, Judy Weleminsky, (in her second starring role?). Helpful, easy watching and recommended.

from 'Community' Summer 1983

BRYAN JONES (22/09/61—27/09/83)
MEMORIAL FUND APPEAL

Bryan Jones who had sickle cell disease and was the Honorary Secretary of the Sickle Cell Society died on 27th September 1983 at the age of 22 due to sudden internal sickling.

Bryan was one of the most active members of our Society; his work was entirely voluntary. He often visited affected families, always giving them comfort and advice. He was an extremely talented artist and put a lot of time and effort into designing the illustrations for our Handbook on sickle cell disease launched in June 1983.

Both the Sickle Cell Society and Bryan's family want to ensure that his work is always remembered by establishing this Memorial Fund.

The Fund will provide resources for people affected by sickle cell disease to further their education in different fields such as art in which Bryan was extremely talented. If enough money is raised we would also like to use it for research into sickle cell disease and to promote awareness of the latest findings possibly through an Annual Memorial Conference.

The Appeal will be launched on Saturday 22nd October 1983 at a "Gala Extravaganza" in Hornsey. We would like to announce the amount raised at our Christmas Party on 17th December 1983.

Bryan's tragic death was a great shock to all who knew and loved him. We do not intend to forget his work for those affected by sickle cell disease and therefore appeal to you to make a generous donation to the Bryan Jones Memorial Fund.

*   *   *

All donations, however small, will be acknowledged. If you would like to organise a fund raising event please contact

CLAUDETTE GRIFFITHS
Sickle Cell Society, c/o Brent Community Health Council, 16 High Street, Harlesden NW10 4LX. Telephone 01-451 3293.

THANK YOU!

BRYAN JONES MEMORIAL FUND

NAME ....

ADDRESS ....

AMOUNT ENCLOSED £............................. DATE ....

95

THE FUND-RAISING ALPHABET

A.   APPEAL
        ART EXHIBITION (OF MEMBERS' WORK)
        ATHLETIC EVENTS or FIELD DAY

B.   BABYSITTING
        A BALL
        BALLOON RACE
        BARBECUE
        BARN DANCE
        BEETLE DRIVE
        BINGO
        BRING-AND-BUY SALE
        BULB GROWING CONTEST

        BUY-A-BRICK
        If you are trying to raise money for a building project ask local people to
        buy-a-brick in the new building for a set price (e.g. £1). Money to equip
        the building can be raised on the same principle, by asking people to
        'buy' items on a shopping list (e.g. '£5 will buy a chair', '£30 will buy a
        slide for the playgroup' etc.).

C.   CABARET
        CARNIVAL
        CAROL SINGING
        CAR WASHING
        CHARITY CRICKET MATCHES
        COFFEE MORNING
        COINS IN A FOUNTAIN
        CONCERT

D.   DANCES
        DINNER

        DOUBLE YOUR MONEY
        Each person is given a sum of money and asked to find a way of
        multiplying it. (e.g. buying a tin of boot polish and starting a shoeshine
        service). A prize is given to the most original and/or profitable idea.
        This is particularly appropriate as an activity for children and youth
        groups.

        DUTCH AUCTION
        Items to be auctioned should be objects which 'everyone' wants (e.g.
        electrical household goods, etc.). The auctioneer takes one item and asks
        what he/she is bid. The first person might say '50p'. The money bid is
        collected in a tin. The next person raises the bid to perhaps 80p and
        must put the **difference** (i.e. 80p - 50p = 30p) into the tin. This process
        continues until the auctioneer suddenly says 'sold', at a time decided in
        advance and known only to him. The buyer has then paid out only a

small sum (perhaps only 40p) for an item worth very much more, since he only pays the difference from the last bidding. The attraction of this event is that anyone who is bidding stands to get the item for a very small outlay, while the auctioneer can make as much as 20 times the actual value of the item.

E. EMPTIES
Collecting and returning empty bottles for the deposit will not only raise money for the organisation, but will help clean up the neighbourhood and aid re-cycling.

EXHIBITIONS

F. FAIRS
FESTIVALS
FETE or GALA
FILM SHOWS
FISHING TOURNAMENT
FLOWER SHOW
FOOTBALL MATCH
FORTUNE TELLING

FRIENDS OF THE ASSOCIATION
Invite local notables and wealthy people to come to a meeting. Get a well-known speaker to outline the work of the organisation and ask those present to form a Friends Group to raise money on your behalf. Make sure, however, that your letter of invitation is quite explicit and leaves no shocks or embarrassment for those who come to the meeting.

FUR AND FEATHER SALE

50-50 SALE
Ask people to contribute nearly new clothes or household articles in good condition on a 'sale or return' basis. If the item is sold, half of the price is returned to the donor, and the other half is kept by the organisation. It is important that the sale price should be agreed in advance with the donor and clearly marked on the item.

G. GARDENING
GARDEN PARTIES
GO-KARTING

H. HALLOWEEN PARTY
HAT SALES

HITCHING BOX
If your members regularly give lifts to friends or hitchhikers ask them to place a collecting box on the dashboard for contributions to your organisation.

HOME DECORATIONS
HOME MADE GOODS

I. INTERNATIONAL EVENING

J. JOBS ABOUT THE HOUSE, GARDEN OR NEIGHBOURHOOD
JUMBLE SALES

K. KIOSKS
Build your own mobile kiosk to sell refreshments, sweets etc., at the roadside or at local events. Once built, the kiosk can be used over and over again and may also have other uses (e.g. publicising your cause). Permission must be obtained for the sale of food stuffs and for street trading.

L. LAWN MOWING

LECTURE SERVICE
If any of your members are regularly invited to give talks to other groups, or lecture in a voluntary capacity, ask them to request a donation for your organisation. For many groups, this is an established way of showing their gratitude to a speaker.

M. MARKET STALL
MEDIEVAL BANQUETS OR FAIRS
MODEL MAKING
MODEL RAILWAY/AIRCRAFT EXHIBITIONS

N. NEARLY NEW SALE

O. OUTGROWN CLOTHES SALE
OUTINGS

P. PAGEANTS
PANEL GAMES
PANTOMIME
PILE OR JAR OF PENNIES
PLANT SALE
POOL TABLES
PRAM RACE
PUPPETRY

PHOTO FLASH
Photographic enthusiasts may take pictures at an event and develop and print them for sale to the subjects. A polaroid camera allows for instant sales at parties, dances etc., but the higher price may cut down the profit margin.

Q. QUIZZES

R. RAFFLES
RALLIES

RECORD SWOPS
RETAILING OF GOODS BOUGHT WHOLESALE

S. SALE OF WORK
SECONDHAND MARKET
SNOWBALL TEA or COFFEE MORNING
SPONSORED EVENTS
SPORTS DAYS
STREET COLLECTIONS
SWIMMING GALA
SWOP SHOP

T. TOMBOLA

TOLL GATE
Set up a 'mock-up' toll gate on the major roads leading in and out of your community and erect a large sign requesting drivers to stop and pay a 'toll' to your organisation. Days when traffic is light and drivers are out for leisure are best (i.e. Sundays). Remember to get police permission.

TOY MAKING
TRADING STAMPS
TREASURE HUNT

U. UNIVERSAL AUNTS
A group who will do anything and go anywhere, odd jobs, busking, decorating, car washing, dog walking, babysitting – in fact anything to raise funds. Add a couple of free services like prescription fetching or shopping for the elderly and infirm to build public sympathy for the group. An appropriate activity for a group of younger members.

V. VALENTINE DANCE
VEGETABLE MARKET
VENDING MACHINES

W. WASTE COLLECTION
There is a wide range of waste materials that can be collected and sold for scrap – paper, metal, old clothes, etc. Check the Yellow Pages under Waste Paper and Scrap Metal Merchants.

WHIST DRIVES
WINDOW CLEANING

X. XMAS CARD SALES
XMAS DRAW

Y. YOUR OWN IDEAS

Z. ZANY IDEAS
Bed races, tramps' suppers, sponsored silences etc.

from 'The Community Organisations' Survival Kit', NFCO

8 PUBLICITY

▷ **How important is publicity?**
▷ **What sort of publicity is appropriate?**
▷ **The job of your publicity officer**
▷ **Producing publicity material**
▷ **How do you approach the media?**

MACCLESFIELD
WOMENS' AID

Watch
this
Space

▷How important is publicity?

Good publicity is vital to every voluntary organisation – for raising funds, recruiting volunteers and members, and informing the general public of your aims and activities. But not **all** publicity is good publicity: you need to remain in control and get across the message **you** want.

The importance you attach to publicity and the type of publicity you seek will vary according to the aims of your organisation. The Sickle Cell Society places great emphasis on it because one of their aims is to increase public awareness of the disease, especially amongst the medical profession. This is reflected in the style and content of their publicity material. On the other hand most of Feltham Community Association's publicity is geared towards attracting people to use the Centre. So they are concerned to produce bright, cheerful posters advertising their social events.

▷What sort of publicity is appropriate?

What do you want to achieve from your publicity?

When planning your publicity it is often easier to start at the end and think about what you want to happen as a result of it.

Ask Yourself	For Example
Who do you want to reach?	Potential members; people in similar circumstances; professional workers; only local people or the nation?
Why do you want to reach them?	Because your membership is declining; to increase public awareness in general; to inform people with similar problems of the services of your group?
What do you want them to do?	Take up your campaign in their part of the country; join your organisation; raise funds on your behalf?

How to reach that audience?

Try to build up a portrait of the type of person you are trying to reach. Consider:

● what papers are they likely to read?

● what places are they likely to visit?

● what television and radio programmes are they likely to watch and listen to?

● what age group are they?

● are they likely to be more affected by hard facts or illustrative examples, like numbers of people suffering from sickle cell anaemia and medical descriptions of the various types of sickle cell disease, or a couple of personal histories of sufferers? Look at the examples of different methods of presentation on the next pages.

What image do you want to present to them?

The group as a whole has to decide what image it wants to present to the public – conforming or trendy, outspoken or conservative, and so on.

Perhaps the best place to begin is by looking at yourselves and asking

● what attracted you to the group?

● how do you see yourselves?

● how would you like the public to see you?

● how do these viewpoints fit in with the stated aims of the group?

Sometimes you will want to vary the image of the group to meet a particular situation. For example, you may never have been involved in local or national politics, but now a particular issue such as youth unemployment or closure of a local health centre will have such a serious impact on your members that you can't avoid becoming involved and being outspoken on this issue. Or you may want to recruit a particular type of volunteer and need to alter your image in order to make these people feel more at home in the organisation.

If you change your public image you will need to be aware of

What causes Sickle cell anaemia?

There are over 300 different types of haemoglobin. The most common type is haemoglobin A (Hb A) and most people inherit Hb A from both parents (Hb AA). Sickle cell anaemia occurs when most of the haemoglobin in the red cells is **sickle haemoglobin** (Hb S). It is given this name because it causes the red blood cells to become sickle or crescent-shaped when they give up oxygen.

What is Sickle cell trait? (Hb AS)

Sickle cell trait occurs when one parent passes on the usual haemoglobin (Hb A) and the other parent passes on sickle haemoglobin (Hb S), resulting in Hb AS. Sickle cell trait is **not** an illness (although very occasionally haematuria may occur). However, if both parents are carriers of Sickle cell trait, there is a one in four chance that each of their children could be born with Sickle cell anaemia. You may find this chart helpful when you explain how sickle haemoglobin is inherited.

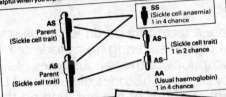

AS
Parent
(Sickle cell trait)

AS
Parent
(Sickle cell trait)

SS
(Sickle cell anaemia)
1 in 4 chance

AS
AS
(Sickle cell trait)
1 in 2 chance

AA
(Usual haemoglobin)
1 in 4 chance

Someone who has Sickle cell trait (⬛
sickle haemoglobin (Hb S) on to their ⬛
the usual haemoglobin (Hb A). But so⬛
(Hb SS) passes sickle haemoglobin (⬛
inherits sickle haemoglobin from bo⬛
anaemia (Hb SS).

What are Haemoglobi⬛
Sickle cell β-thalassa⬛

These conditions occur when som⬛
from one of their parents and eith⬛
the other parent. The symptoms ⬛
but usually less severe than, thos⬛
cell anaemia and people with Ha⬛
problems with sight or with thro⬛
Sickle cell β-thalassaemia.

Who gets Sickle cell anaemia?

In Britain, Sickle cell anaemia is most common in people of African or West Indian (Caribbean) descent. (1 in 10 have Sickle cell trait and 1 in 400 have Sickle cell anaemia). It may also occur in people from the Eastern Mediterranean, the Middle East, India and Pakistan. This geographical distribution has probably arisen because Sickle cell trait offers some protection against malaria. (Sickle cell anaemia does **not** offer this protection).

What are the symptoms of Sickle cell anaemia?

Although Sickle cell anaemia is present from birth, symptoms are rare before the age of three to six months. The main symptoms of Sickle cell anaemia are episodes of anaemia, pain or infection. These are called **crises**. Some people get crises quite often, others may only have them once every several years. In between crises the person is usually quite well.

A crisis is a sudden worsening of any of the following:

Pain Sickle cell anaemia sometimes causes attacks of pain to the chest, abdomen, back, jaw, legs and arms. They occur because the sickling of the red blood cells causes them to block up small blood vessels and stop the flow of blood. Some people get painful crises quite often, others may only have them once several years. The 'sickling' of red blood cells which can cause a crisis is more likely to take place under certain conditions. These include a reduction of the level of oxygen in the blood (after exertion, during some anaesthetics or at very high altitudes); dehydration; and during pregnancy. Painful crises may also occur in association with febrile childhood or adult illnesses. If the pain is very severe, admission to hospital may be necessary.

Anaemia People with Sickle cell anaemia are always anaemic. This may cause them to become tired or short of breath after exercise. The anaemia may become worse as a result of acute splenic sequestration or an aplastic crisis. If so, emergency treatment with blood transfusions may be necessary.

Infections People with Sickle cell anaemia are particularly prone to minor infections and also to serious and life-threatening infections like septicaemia, pneumococcal meningitis and osteomyelitis.

Other problems Sickle cell anaemia is a multi-system disorder. Children may get painful inflammation of the hands and feet (called the hand-foot syndrome). They are also prone to enuresis and delayed puberty. Adults (and sometimes children) can develop stiff and painful joints or ulcers on the lower legs. In general, people with Sickle cell anaemia have an increased incidence of gallstones, jaundice, haematuria, strokes, priapism and difficulties during pregnancy and childbirth.

(Note: People who only have Sickle cell **trait** do not suffer any of the symptoms of Sickle cell **anaemia**).

The facts about Sickle Cell disease (extract from SCS's guide for GPs, nurses and other health professionals).

MY LIFE STORY OF SICKLE-CELL ANAEMIA

My name is Laurel, I am 13 years old and I was born on December 26, Boxing Day. It was not until I was 4 or 5 till my parents knew that I had sickle-cell anaemia. When I was small I didn't attend hospital as much as now, thinking back to when I was small I can see the ward, and me in a cot, I can see my mum pushing me and my sister in a push-chair out of the hospital.

As the days and months went past I didn't get any better or worst, it was just the same no real improvement no worse improvement. Later on my mother was told that my brother had it as well. Now that I am 13 years old I am not at all scared of sickle-cell anaemia, I can't say I'm brave but I know all about it and know how to live with it. It isn't something that you can throw away and not care about it, but it's something you must care about.

The only thing I don't like about it is that it stops you doing what teenagers do, I can't do athletics, can't go to disco's in winter because it's cold, and I can't expose myself. I do hate missing school and staying in hospital for weeks. It's like being

Of the four siblings, only Laurel (centre) and Geoffrey have sickle-cell disease.

shut up in a world by yourself, it's boring and it gets you thinking about how you're going to fight it and live with it for the rest of your life.

I suffer a lot with horrible aching pains in my joints. When they say "You'll need a drip Laurel" I know what it means.

When I get pains I can't walk, I just lie in bed. Anyhow I cope with it and live with it and still get on happily in life. It's not what people think it's like, but I know what it's like and I'll always know what it's like.

Laurel

SELF-HELP IN SICKLE-CELL ANAEMIA

Elizabeth Anionwu describes the formation in Brent of a self-help group for victims of sickle-cell anaemia.

Elizabeth Anionwu
a community nurse tutor in the
Brent Health District.

It has become increasingly clear that conventional medical and nursing care is not meeting all the needs of individuals and families affected by sickle-cell anaemia. Towards the end of 1976, several of us in the Brent Health District including myself (with a cousin who suffers from the disease) and the haematologist (who has recently arrived and was struck by the large number of cases) were becoming increasingly concerned.

Traditional forms of care concentrate too much on the physical aspects of sickle-cell anaemia rather than on the social and emotional ones. By this I mean an emphasis on diagnosis and subsequent treatment of the sickling crisis, with little counselling, support or health education in between. Most health workers I have met know little about the condition and seem to believe that nothing much can be done to ameliorate its eventual outcome. Many feel that the prognosis is poor. Yet Lehmann and Huntsmann in
continued

A personal view (extract from 'World Medicine', 21/9/77.

the possible consequences. For example, by changing the style of the group will you lose more members than you gain? Are you going to anger your funders by voicing your members' problems and concerns? This is a common dilemma for community groups. How you resolve such conflicts depends on the particular circumstances, the aims of your group and its current image.

In general, though, it is unwise to rush to the press at the drop of a hat. Think first of other ways in which the situation can be resolved. You do not have to lose sight of your principles but they may save you getting egg on your face, and so losing credibility. This way you will make a greater impact with your chosen issues and you will be taken more seriously by public and press alike.

Of course there will be occasions when bold and decisive action such as getting up a petition or lobbying your M.P. is essential. These can be effective – and free – methods of getting publicity for your organisation. A useful pamphlet describing how to go about petitioning and lobbying is available from Inter-action, and other useful booklets on this subject are listed in Chapter 12, 'Resources'.

How will you deal with the response to your publicity?

Be sure you can back up and support your publicity campaigns. For example, if you are advertising on your local radio station for more volunteers, make sure that someone is available for the next couple of weeks to answer the phone number you give in the broadcast – and make sure that person knows what

£100,000 a year is available to groups in the transmission area of Television South – TVS. Their Trust makes one-off grants and has established a good record in helping provide facilities of all sorts in community centres. Grants range from under £50 to nearly £5,000. Details TRVSTVS, 60/61 Buckingham Gate, London SW1.

from 'Community' Spring 1983

information to give prospective volunteers. If you are in an advice-giving group make sure you have a good supply of any leaflets mentioned in your publicity and that there are people available to send out these leaflets.

If you are asked to take part in a radio or television programme which is likely to result in a demand for your leaflets, don't forget to ask the producers of the programme to contribute towards the cost of the print-run. They may also be willing to give you a donation for contributing to the programme.

- decide who you want to reach and what you want them to do as a result of your publicity.
- list all the outlets of publicity likely to be used by this type of person.
- decide what image you want to present which will attract them to your organisation.
- check you can cope with the response.

▷ The job of your publicity officer

To a large extent every member of your group is its publicity officer, when they are talking to their friends, families and work-mates. But most voluntary and community groups find it convenient and beneficial to appoint one person, or sometimes a small sub-committee depending on the size of the group and range of activities, who will be responsible for co-ordinating publicity campaigns.

Make checklists and mailing lists:

● **members** – name, address, telephone number, position in group, if any, useful skills

> Mary Stevens, 24 Barlow Way, Anytown. Tel. 29786.
> Member of fund-raising committee.
> Willing to distribute leaflets, house-to-house, street.

● **distributors** – people or organisations which are willing to take a poster in their shop/office window. This list may include schools, colleges, local shops, factories, offices, local authority departments, information centres, local libraries, sports halls or senior citizens clubs.

> Anytown Building Society, High Street, Anytown. Tel. 57984.
> Contact: Mr. Roberts, Manager. Willing to put A3 poster in window for fund-raising events.

● local printers, advertising agents, stationers – name, address, telephone number, services, costs:

> Babcock Printers Ltd., 123 Anywhere Road, Anytown. Tel. 45678.
> Contact: Mr. P. Brown. Asst. Manager.
> Service: Stationery & Photocopying.
> Prices (July 1983): A4 White £2.20 per ream. Copy - 10p per sheet A4.

● Newspapers, magazines, radio and television stations – name, address and telephone number, relevant programmes, regular features, names of news editors and sympathetic reporters or programme presenters:

> Anytown Radio, Faraway House, London Rd., Anytown. Tel. 12345.
> News Editor: Mike Jones.
> "Anytown Community" - weekly, Monday 7.30pm. (local news about voluntary groups, 2 minute slots for groups, panel about local issues).
> Presenter: Jane Wells.

Besides getting to know people in the media it is also a good idea to make contact with local printers, stationers etc. who may be able to let you have end-of-stock items cheaply, or off-cuts of paper. You can approach managers of local firms who have their own print departments to see if they would do the work cheaply for you, or do the artwork for your posters. There may be a local community resource centre, such as Feltham Community Resource Centre, in your area which will print your work more cheaply than a commercial printer, or run a stationery purchasing consortium. Your local CVS or Community Association will be able to tell you if a centre exists in your town.

Try to find out if members of your organisation have any particular interests or skills which may be helpful to you, such as photography, making up crosswords or typing. Other members may work at a local printer's and be able to enlist the support of their employers to help you. Make a list of volunteers willing to help you with the mundane tasks of duplicating, handing out leaflets, sticking down envelopes, and so forth, which will give you more time to concentrate on the task which is described next.

The best method of keeping these lists is to use a card index. It is vital that all your lists are kept up to date and checked every six months or so. Don't forget to remove old cards!

Develop contacts

As you will have noticed from the above examples, it is helpful if you have the name of an individual you can contact for assistance. It is better still if you can put a face to that name!

To begin with you will need to listen and watch all relevant radio and television programmes and note how they present their material. Are they interested in particular sorts of events or people? How are interviews done? Do they have a panel of speakers, or do they prefer to do individual interviews. Do they give community groups a few minutes to state their own case? Study the local papers and magazines and note down any regular columns that tackle community issues and the way these stories are presented.

Make a note of the names of any reporters or presenters who consistently deal with community issues. Write to them asking for an appointment to discuss the work of your group and how they might help you with publicity. Most reporters and presenters are only too pleased to have regular contacts within community groups so you are helping them as much as yourselves.

The publicity officer is a key member of the organisation. They need to be fully aware of all the group's aims and activities and to be good at, and enjoy, talking and writing.

The publicity officer should not be the only member who writes letters to the local papers, gives television and radio interviews, or spends hours behind the duplicator. But it is their job to develop contacts with the media, plan the publicity and enlist the support of other members in achieving those plans.

The tasks of the publicity officer can be divided roughly into four areas:

Planning and co-ordinating a campaign

You don't need to have a large budget to run a very successful publicity campaign. Nor do you have to be a public relations expert.

Know what resources are available

The key to success is knowing exactly what resources are available to you and using those resources to best effect. A few carefully produced posters in the right places will have much more impact than tatty bits of paper scattered about all over the place. Put quality before quantity.

Look for free publicity

Examine the group itself to see how you can get free publicity. What have you got?

● **yourselves:** members will talk about the group to their family and friends so new members must always be made warmly welcome. And all members must be kept informed about the group's aims and activities so they can pass on this information.

● **members' children** – can you organise special events for them or start a junior club? How can they help with fund-raising at school or in their neighbourhood? Stories about children are always popular with the media.

● **the group's activities:** what events are planned? Why are these being organised? Are you doing any surveys in the neighbourhood? Keep yourself informed of all that is going on in the group and in your area so that you can join in with town shows, community centre open days and so forth.

─ Sunshine tea party ─

West Watford CA's Street Party was held in celebration of Community Day.

Some 130 children sat down to tea on a gloriously sunny afternoon. There was a fancy dress competition, a gymnastic display by children from one of the local schools, a Police van for the children to inspect, young people from the hospital radio service, and two clowns who kept the party going.

Photo courtesy Evening Post Echo.

from 'Community' Autumn 1983

● **the group's facilities:** if you have an office or centre try to organise events there. Be sure to keep it clean, tidy and welcoming! Invite local reporters to visit and tell them what you do at your premises.

These can all provide sources of free publicity – all you have to do is write a short press release and send it to the people on your media mailing list.

Allow plenty of time

Finally, you have to carefully plan your campaign, allowing yourself plenty of time to get posters printed and distributed, and press releases written. A hurried campaign will result in mistakes and shortcomings.

The job of the publicity officer is continuous. Although there may be particular occasions for which an increase in publicity is required, you should always be looking at the group itself and keeping a watchful overview of its public image so that the groundwork is well established for when you need to attract some special publicity.

■ get to know all you can about your organisation's members, aims and activities.

■ keep up-to-date lists of local printers, stationers, media contacts, members, and distributors.

■ get to know useful people in the media – local reporters, programme producers etc. – and keep them informed of your activities.

■ examine the organisation itself for free sources of publicity.

■ allow yourself plenty of time to produce and distribute your publicity material.

▷ Producing publicity material

Even if you exploit to the full all your free sources of publicity, there will still be occasions when you have to pay for printing and other work. But there are ways of making a limited budget go a long way by planning and taking care with everything you produce. This section outlines the most popular and effective forms of publicity material used by community groups.

The key points to remember when producing any publicity material are to keep it: **SIMPLE, BRIEF, ACCURATE, POSITIVE, ENTHUSIASTIC and SINCERE.** These rules apply equally to posters, leaflets and press releases.

Newsletter

A monthly or quarterly newsletter to members helps keep them informed about what the group is doing. You can also send it to news editors on your local papers and radio stations,

ST. HELENS and DISTRICT HANDICAPPED CHILDRENS TRUST

CHAIRMAN
Dr.J.A.Sills M.A.,M.B.,B.Chir.
M.R.C.P.(U.K.),D.C.H.
23,Kennedy Park Lane,
Prescot
L.N 3FA
Tel. 051 426 3161

HONORARY SECRETARY
Mrs A.Eaves,
8,Henrity Prescott,
Newton in Willows
Tel. Newton 4331

NEWSLETTER No. 4, JULY, 1982
ABOUT THE TRUST

The Trust was set up in April last year, following several meetings between concerned professionals and parents who considered needs of handicapped children and their families living in the St. Helens Metropolitan District and how services could be improved.

From the beginning, it has been an exciting venture in that it has involved complete co-operation between voluntary and statutory bodies. In view of the current financial constraints upon Local Authority and Area Health Authority budgets it would seem that an independent charitable body such as this will have a considerable part to play in any future expansion of services to handicapped children and their families.

The aim of the Trust is, therefore, to offer help and support to every family in the St. Helens District who has a handicapped child.

CONTINUING PROJECTS

(a)   INFORMATION GUIDE FOR PARENTS
The information guide is available for all parents of handicapped children living in the area of the St. Helens Metropolitan District. Although this guide has been widely distributed, there may be some parents or professional and voluntary bodies who have been unavoidably overlooked. This can be remedied, by requesting a copy from Roy Ashurst, Town Hall, Market Street, Newton-Le-Willows. Tel: Newton 5121.

The Committee may be looking at the possibility of re-printing the Guide in April/May next year, two years following the first issue and it is therefore vital that information in the Guide should be correct and constantly up-dated. In order to do this, any new groups, changes of officals or helpful information should be notified to Roy Ashurat (NLW 5121) so that the quality and correctness of information can be maintained.

(b)   NEWTON OPPORTUNITY GROUP
This group, set up in November, 1980 for mothers and their children with handicaps, continues to thrive. It meets on Monday and Thursday mornings each week, with an average attendance of 18 children with their mums. On 13th May, the Group transferred to other accommodation at the Legh Street (St. Johns) Parish Hall. A large 'container' has been obtained to use for storage of equipment and other uses which will serve as an 'extension' to the building. Volunteer drivers are an essential part of the Service and are always needed. Voluntary help at the group is also always welcome. Please contact Mrs. Margaret Caterall. Tel: Ashton-in-Makerfield 726774. A lot of community interest is being shown and given to the Opportunity Group. Thanks are due to Haydock High School who send two pupils every Monday morning to help with the children. At Christmas time, several pupils from the school entertained the children and distributed sweets. The school also presented the Group with a wooden climbing frame and tunnel which the children are delighted with. Students from courses held at the Newton College of Education also attend morning sessions and give valuable help and the tutors also show great interest and give help and support.

MUMS SUPPORT GROUP

This group was started recently, mainly for mothers of young children who may be attending Special Schools. The group meet every Wednesday

-2-

morning from 10 - 12 a.m. at the YMCA buil
St. Helens. Opportunity is given for moth
to have a chat and a coffee and generally
helpful information etc. The group is on
moment, but anyone interested in joining
Williams - St. Helens 818694 or Mrs. Lind

ANNUAL GENERAL MEETING

The A.G.M. of the Trust was held at the
April, 1982 when about 40 people attende

The following officers were appointed fo

Chairman   Dr. John Sills

Vice Chairman   Mr. Leon Maguire

Secretary   Mrs. Ann Eaves

Treasurer   Mr. Tony Scott

Committee

The Chairman thanked all members for
a new Committee was elected, which inc
Newton Opportunity Group and parents.

The three Sub-Committees (Playgroup,
and Resources) will continue to funct
members and helpers are always welco

Former Secretary

The Chairman, in his report, referre
done by the first and former Secreta
resigned from the honorary position.

Discussion Group

Following the business of the meeti
discussions took place, in three gr
the Trust and suggestions for new
the discussions, the most importan

1.   Holiday Play Schemes. It w
     efforts should be made to e
     short holiday periods (i.e.
     long Summer holidays. This
     Parents and Friends of Ment
     basis, with much success, b
     cash will be required to ex
     and their families.

     It was pointed out that th
     offered to mentally handic
     specifically for children
     this gap may be filled and
     short-term play scheme and
     facility proves successfu

2.   Baby-sitting Service. Se
     parents to be given occas
     service; although many pa
     with volunteers who may t
     was felt the best way to meet thr
     groups with their handicapped child, to try to 'exchange'
     other an occasional night out, etc. If any parent feels they need
     and welcome a baby-sitter they are advised to contact any member of
     the Trust who will try to help, if possible.

councillors, your MP and any others you feel it is politic to keep informed of your work.

For the Sickle Cell Society and the St. Helens & District Handicapped Childrens' Trust the newsletter is the main vehicle for keeping their members and supporters in touch with each other, using it to pass on useful tips of information and to advertise fund-raising and social events.

With the increasing availability of electronic stencil cutters at secretarial agencies, students' unions and community resource centres, it is possible to produce cheap but attractive duplicated leaflets with bold headings and cartoons. Plain paper photocopiers can also be used but this will be more expensive unless you only require a couple of dozen copies. The text should be laid out in two or three columns down the page as this is read more easily than lines of text spread across the whole page; it should be broken up into small sections with bold headings.

Worldwide distribution

Scunthorpe Federation of CA's publishes a newsletter, FACT, that is sent to well-wishers all over the globe. Two expatriates showed FACT around a large quarterly meeting of Californian community workers who pronounced the newsletter to be of exceptionally high standard.

from 'Community' Spring 1983

Community newspaper

This may be an extension of the newsletter, or a newspaper in its own right, with copies being delivered to every household in the neighbourhood. Obviously, it will cost a lot more to produce and you will probably need an editorial group to ensure it is printed regularly. You can reduce costs by obtaining advertisements from local shops and firms, and making a charge for the paper. A grant may be available from your local council to help with printing costs.

Leaflets

Again, these can be produced attractively and cheaply with the aid of an electronic stencil cutter and use of an extra colour. Like the newsletter it should be well-spaced with bold headings and kept brief but accurate.

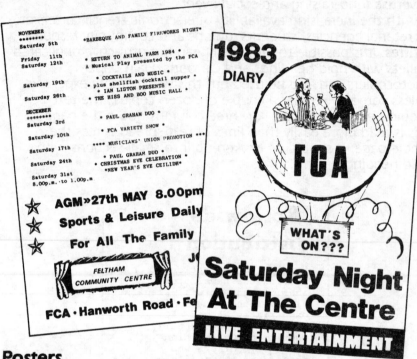

Posters

These can be produced cheaply using silk-screen techniques. Your local art college may be able to help you with these or they may organise training sessions. If not, why don't you suggest to them, or your local adult education officer, that they arrange an evening class.

Think about where your posters will be displayed, the image they will create and the most appropriate size for displaying in shops, or on noticeboards. Always make sure the name of your organisation, the date, time and place of the event is clear. It is a good idea to have your posters checked for spelling mistakes – and always check the day of the week against the date! Another point to consider is whether the quality of paper is suitable for outdoors – you can cover ordinary cardboard with

protective film. Use spirit felt pens, rather than water which run
and blot, and remember to remove old posters when the event
is over.

Poster contest

Maybank C.A. in East London
are organising a poster
competition for local young
people. They want a poster
to publicise their community
care scheme, Maycare. To
help the designer, they give
the following examples of
their work: collecting a
prescription, doing an
invalid's shopping, helping
a consumer make a complaint,
talking to a depressed man,
going for a walk with a woman
who is afraid to go out alone,
babysitting while a mother
collected a prescription for
a sick child, taking someone
to a hospital appointment.

from 'Community' Spring 1982

Display boards

If you are lucky enough to have a display board on or close to
your premises be sure to state the name of the organisation,
keep it tidy with up-to-date notices and try to make it exciting
and interesting, perhaps with photographs of members, and
well-produced posters. Re-paint and repair the board regularly.
If you want to have permanent street signposts to your centre
you will need to get permission from your local Council's
planning department.

Slide tape, film and video

If your group intends arranging talks to schools, local clubs and
others in the community, it is often helpful to have some visual
displays. Still photographs are the most obvious choice but these
get damaged or lost and can interrupt the flow of your talk
while they are passed around. Slides are better but you will
need a projector and screen.

To make a slide-tape you will need a good 35mm camera, a
projector and screen, and a tape recorder. Slide tapes are effective,
relatively easy to produce, and copies can be made. But the
amount of equipment involved may not make it feasible. The same
applies to film and video, which are far more costly. There are,
however, film workshops which may be able to make a film for
you, or you may be able to borrow equipment from a local

school or college. The local photographic club may be persuaded to make a film for you and lend equipment. You should include all these contacts in your checklist for resources.

Other popular forms of publicity material include car-stickers, badges, balloons carrying your own message, loud hailers, audio-tapes, and so on... and on... The list is as long as your imagination allows it to be!

■ be imaginative!

■ keep your publicity: SIMPLE, BRIEF, ACCURATE, POSITIVE and ENTHUSIASTIC.

■ think about where your publicity material will be displayed.

▷ How do you approach the media?

Newspapers and magazines

Most towns have at least two local or regional newspapers. As suggested earlier, the publicity officer should carefully study several copies of each of these looking for appropriate regular features and names of reporters.

Radio

The BBC has four national radio services (Radios 1, 2, 3 and 4). Listen out for programmes produced as current affairs magazine programmes (Checkpoint, Woman's Hour) and others by the Continuing Education Unit, Radio, which produces programmes of interest to voluntary groups.

There are also some 30 BBC local radio stations and over 40 independent radio stations. Details of all stations and the areas they cover are contained in the BBC and IBA handbooks — copies available from most public libraries. The Media Project's **Directory of Social Action Programmes** lists details of most social action programmes.

Besides giving out news of a purely local nature, local radio stations also get national stories and may contact you to ask for the local view on these national events. You could even make your own response to a national story by phoning in and talking to the news editor. One advantage radio has over newspapers and television is that it is on the air all day and you can phone in at any time to make an urgent appeal.

Television

BBC television programmes are usually transmitted across the UK with only a few slots for regional programming. The BBC departments which will be most helpful to you are the Community Programme Unit and the Continuing Education Department, TV.

ITV is divided across 14 transmission regions which means there is greater opportunity for regional programming. Some ITV companies also have a Public Service Announcement scheme. These are slots for community groups and are organised by groups of community agencies in each region. Most ITV companies now have Continuing and Community Education Officers and you should make contact with your local officer.

Details of BBC Television and ITV transmission regions and relevant departments are contained in the BBC and IBA handbooks.

Channel 4 does not make programmes itself but commissions them from independent producers and ITV companies. There are sometimes opportunities for voluntary organisations to become involved in making and following up programmes for Channel 4.

The Media Project

This organisation is an information service run by the Volunteer Centre and its aim is to keep voluntary organisations up-to-date with broadcasting opportunities. If your organisation is intending to make much use of the media it is worthwhile taking out a subscription for £7.50 per year.

Writing a press release

A press release, or 'news release' is a summary of facts and views or both. Some examples are given on the next few pages. Amongst the points to note from these examples are:

● a press release should be short, sharp and to the point – who, what, when, where, and why.

● quotes add life to a story and strength to the opinions they contain but make sure they are relevant and not too rambling.

● find a good, short headline – maximum five words.

● summarise the main points in the first paragraph.

● give the telephone numbers of members to contact for further information – and make sure these people are available to answer their phone.

● always type the press release in double spacing and with wide margins. If you are sending it to a particular reporter or presenter, be sure to address it to them, and send two copies. Try to keep your releases to one page in length, but if they do go on to two put 'mf' at the bottom of the first page (more follows) and 'end' at the end.

● send out press releases in good time. If you don't want editors to use a story before a certain time or day – perhaps the release is publicising what someone is going to say at a meeting – put at the top of the release the words 'Embargoed until (state day and time)'.

● if possible, send a photograph to local newspapers.

● always keep a copy of the release for yourself. Make a note of the response you receive from reporters. Also, keep records of

SICKLE CELL SOCIETY

c/o Brent Community Health Council,

16, High Street,
Harlesden,
London NW10 4LX

Tel: 01 451 3293

Date:

Registered charity (No. 281154)

P R E S S   R E L E A S E

THE BRYAN JONES MEMORIAL APPEAL FUND

Recently the Sickle Cell Society announced the death of our
Honorary Secretary, Bryan Jones, who died on 27th September
1983 at the age of 22.

On Saturday 22nd October, at a Concert in Hornsey, we launched
'The Bryan Jones Memorial Appeal Fund' in honour of Bryan's
memory. We hope to use the money raised through this fund to
provide scholarships for people with sickle cell disease who
wish to further their education in some way. We also hope to
hold an Annual Conference to discuss the latest findings in
the world of sickle cell disease.

So far we have received £1,292 towards this fund, £1,000 of
which was donated by the TCB company. Donations have also
come from Bryan's family and friends, from a collection at
the Hornsey concert and from Mr Ray Samuel who donated the
royalties from his record "No Cruelty."

Enclosed is a leaflet giving further details of this appeal.
We are asking the public to make a generous donation towards
'The Bryan Jones Memorial Fund' so that we may be able to
offer help to others affected by sickle cell disease in areas
of further education. Bryan was an extremely talented artist
and dedicated to helping fellow sufferers. Both the Sickle
Cell Society and Bryan's family feel that in setting up
this fund we would have met with Bryan's approval if he
were still here today.

* * *

SICKLE CELL DISEASE THE NEED FOR IMPROVED SERVICES

In September of this year the Sickle Cell Society produced
a second edition of the report 'Sickle Cell Disease: The
Need for Improved Services' (a copy of which is enclosed).
When first published in October 1981, this report received
widespread publicity and led to questions on the adequacy of
services, and treatment available to sickle cell sufferers
being asked in the House of Commons. This first edition
has now completely sold out.

The updated report is now available to the public at a cost
of 80p. Further details are available from:

CLAUDETTE GRIFFITHS
on (01) 451 3293

the response you receive from each publicity source. This will help you to gauge their effectiveness.

● if you are appealing for funds, furniture or volunteers, or encouraging people to visit your centre or office, be sure you are geared up to cope with the response.

Interviews

If you make an approach to a broadcasting station you must be prepared for an invitation to take part in an interview. You should think in advance about who will be the most appropriate person to do that interview. It may not always be the chairperson or the publicity officer: you may have to be honest with yourselves and consider which Executive member or other person in the group is most able to answer difficult questions with confidence and an enthusiasm which will encourage the desired response from the viewing and listening public.

There are several training courses in interviewing techniques: some CVS's arrange these locally, and the Media Project provides national courses.

Before taking part in any interview you should find out:

● what is the programme.

● what will you be interviewed about. Ask for a rehearsal first, or run through the questions which will give you a chance to organise your thoughts.

● is it going out live or being recorded?

● how long is the interview?

● will you be interviewed alone, or with someone of opposing views, or as part of a panel?

Again, you must ensure you can provide a full back-up to any requests you make during an interview.

And remember you don't have to say 'Yes' every time you are invited to take part in a programme. This may seem hard at first but if you feel your participation will not benefit your organisation, it is better to say "No thank you, not this time!"

- keep press releases short, sharp and to the point.

- send press releases out in good time.

- always keep a copy yourself and note the response you receive.

- select suitable members for handling radio and television interviews.

- ask the programme producer to go through the questions with you beforehand.

- be sure you can deal with any requests or appeals you make in your publicity.

9 RECRUITING STAFF AND VOLUNTEERS

▷ Do you need staff?
▷ What staff do you need?
▷ Job descriptions
▷ What salary should you pay them?
▷ Recruiting and interviewing
▷ What is a contract of employment?
▷ Is staff training necessary?
▷ Temporary employment schemes

NO, NO, NO, THE JOB DESCRIPTION CALLS
FOR YOU TO LIAISE — NOT LAZE...

First – a note of caution

With the introduction of various government schemes aimed at reducing the impact of unemployment, more and more community groups are becoming employers. Sadly, for some groups and their employees, these arrangements do not work out satisfactorily. If you are considering employing staff on either a permanent basis or under a government temporary employment scheme, you should first think carefully about the responsibility. What is a voluntary job to you will be your employee's livelihood. Whilst you will want to employ someone who has a personal commitment to the work of your group it is unfair to expect them to put that work before their own financial needs and commitment to their families.

▶Do you need staff?

Before rushing out to collect from your local JobCentre an application form for the latest government employment scheme, you should ask yourself the following questions.

● why do you want staff? What is wrong with your present arrangements for using volunteers?

● will paid staff resolve these problems? Or are you looking for a way around a problem rather than tackling the problem itself?

● what precisely will your staff do?

● do you want to continue using volunteers as well and, if so, what impact will the presence of paid staff have on your volunteers?

● who will supervise the employee's work and how will they do it?

● what will be the role of the Executive Committee if there are paid staff? Are your Executive members willing – and able – to take on the exacting duties involved in handling and being accountable for large sums of public money? Is the organisation itself sufficiently strong and stable to take on these responsibilities?

If, after answering all of these questions honestly you and your Executive members still feel employing staff is the solution for your group, then read on!

The pros and cons of employing staff

The days of Lady Bountiful have passed, and few people nowadays are able to give more than a few hours a week to working as a volunteer. Even if you are lucky enough to have amongst your membership someone who is willing to regard their voluntary work as a full-time commitment, that voluntary work is rarely a valid substitute for paid employment, and the chances are that if that person obtained paid work your organisation would be in serious difficulty and unable to find a replacement for a very long time.

Some Pros	Some Cons
Continuity	Places an increased responsibility on the Executive
Greater efficiency, leading to:	
– ability to increase volume of work	Creates more work for some members i.e. Treasurer and Chairperson
– improved public image	
– more time to develop the group's activities	Possibility of losing control of the organisation if too much authority is delegated to staff
Extends the times of day or week that the organisation can function	

▶What staff do you need?

Go back to your earlier thoughts about why you want to employ staff. List those tasks which presently are not being carried out or not being carried out properly.

Probably your list will start with one sweeping statement such as 'To do all the day-to-day running of the Refuge', or 'To carry out all the administration of the Centre'. This wide-ranging statement should then be broken down into specific tasks; for example 'administration of the Centre' will include dealing with routine correspondence, keeping accounts, ordering supplies for the Centre, arranging repairs and so forth.

When you have listed all the tasks which need to be done now, think about ways in which the organisation's work could be developed and extended by the extra time which will be available to you and list these as tasks. For example 'day-to-day running of the Refuge' may include all of the routine

EXAMPLE: MACCLESFIELD WOMEN'S AID STAFF REQUIREMENTS

GROUP	TASK	SKILLS AND QUALITIES	PRIORITY
A	Admitting families	Available odd hours, sympathetic attitude, occasional driving	2
C	Recruiting volunteers	Good verbal and written communications	4
C	Supervising volunteers	Encouraging manner, good organiser	5
A	Counselling and advising women at the Refuge and after they have left	Counselling experience, knowledge of welfare benefits and legal position of battered women	1
A/C	Liaising with government depts. on women's behalf	Good verbal and written communications	3
C	Publicity, giving talks etc	Good verbal and written communications	9
B	Keeping all accounts and paying wages	Knowledge of book-keeping and PAYE	8
C	Writing reports for the Management Committee, government departments and others	Research experience, good written communications	7
A	Arranging and supervising play activities	Experience of working with children	10
B	Typing, taking minutes, general office work	Secretarial qualifications and work experience	11
B	Keeping records	General clerical experience	

administrative tasks listed for the Centre and some developmental tasks, such as 'the provision of after care and support to women and children who have left the Refuge', or 'publicity about the problems which confront battered women'.

Having listed all the tasks which need to be done and all those which you would like to do if only you had the time, you now need to consider how many people will be required to achieve all that and what skills and/or qualifications they will need. It is helpful to place the tasks in an order of priority so that if you are not able to obtain funds for all the staff you need, at least you can ensure that the essential tasks are carried out.

Your list will probably range from tasks which require practical skills, like typing or driving, to those which require personal skills, such as counselling. There will be tasks which require no particular skill or qualification but depend more on practical experience, such as the general administrative chores of ordering goods, control of stocks, arranging repairs.

The next stage is to group the tasks according to the skills required and to assess approximately how much time per week will be required for each task. No doubt you will end up with lots of tasks which at first glance don't fit neatly into any group. If any of those tasks is high on your priority list and is very time-consuming you should look at the problem the other way round: instead of trying to slot this task into an existing group, perhaps it would be better to group other less important jobs around this central task.

Organising your thoughts in this way should produce several job descriptions. No one description should list tasks which total more than 40 hours a week, or which are impossible to fill because the times you require that person to work are absurd, like opening the building at 7.00am and closing it at 1.00am, or because the tasks are so diverse that you will never find anyone with all the skills required – a bar steward who can also type and do the artwork for your newsletter and counsel young people using the centre. Of course you may be lucky and find such a saint, but it is safer to assume you won't.

You should also keep at the back of your mind the value of staff training. For example, it may be that rather than employing two people for a few hours each per week, one to do the book-keeping and another to do general administrative tasks, it would be better to employ one person for all those hours and arrange to train them in the area for which they lack the necessary skills. You need to decide which of the tasks has the greatest priority.

▶ Job descriptions

This is your list of all the tasks which the employee will be expected to perform. You should work out the job description in the way described above **before** you appoint anyone to the post – the person must suit the job, not the job suit the person!

A well-thought out job description is an invaluable aid in the management of staff. Making clear from the start what are your employee's duties prevents friction at a later date. Most people like to know what is expected of them by their employers. And they like to know to whom they are responsible. It is common practice nowadays to send a copy of the job description to applicants so they can see what the job entails and whether it is a job they would like and are able to do.

Here are the job descriptions which the Manpower Services

Commission accepted from Macclesfield Womens' Aid who wanted, and got, under the Community Programme, one full-time project manager, two part-time project officers, and one part-time clerical officer.

Macclesfield Women's Aid.
objective... to provide a refuge for battered women and children

Job Title: Project Manager

Employer: Macclesfield Women's Aid Management Committee

Location: As required by the employer

Duties: Overall supervision of the day to day running of the Refuge including:

- supervision of the project's staff

- admission of families to the Refuge

- referring women to appropriate agencies and professionals

- recruiting and organising the work of volunteers

- generally providing sympathetic support and advice to women staying at the Refuge and after they have left

- Liaising with local government departments and others about the requirements of the women in the Refuge

- publicity and promotion of the Project

- ensure any delegated financial transactions are correct and that the correct wages for hours of work are paid.

- Report on the progress of the Refuge to the Management Committee

- Contribute to the continued development of the resource

- undertake other duties as required by Macclesfield Women's Aid

Responsible to: Macclesfield Women's Aid Management Committee

Conditions of service: As laid down in the enclosed documents

---

Job Title: Clerical Officer (part-time)

Employer: Macclesfield Women's Aid Management Comm

Location: as required by the employer

Duties: To provide clerical support to the Proje

- keeping the Projects' accounts

- calculation and payment of wages

- paying any income in to the bank

- typing, photocopying, duplicating, filing, maintenance of records

- recording minutes of meetings between management and staff

- liaising closely with the Projects' treasurer

- if, after carrying out these duties there is sufficient time, assisting with the day to day running of the Refuge

- to contribute to the continued development of this resource

- to undertake other duties as required by Maccles...

Responsible to: Project Manager on be

Conditions of Service: As laid down in

Job Title: Part-time Project Officer

Employer: Macclesfield Women's Aid Management Committee

Location: as required by the Employer

Duties: To be involved with the day to day running of the Refuge, including

- assist with admissions of families and generally provide sympathetic support to them whilst they are staying at the Refuge and after they have left

- assist with play activities for the children whilst in the Refuge

- liaising with other agencies on behalf of and together with the women

- to contribute to the continued development of this resource

- to undertake other duties as required by Macclesfield Womens Aid

Responsible to: The Project Manager on Behalf of the Management Committee

Conditions of Service: As laid down in the enclosed documents

A popular format for job descriptions is to begin with a statement of the broad objectives of the post, and then to give a breakdown of the major tasks. The broad objective can be used in the advertisement for the post.

Usually it is unnecessary to list all the activities which are included in one task, such as counting the cash each day, writing the names of the payees in the book, issuing receipts, banking the money, writing out cheques and so on – otherwise your job descriptions would run to several pages!

Some job descriptions give additional information such as the

---

Title: Secretary, the Sickle Cell Society

Grade: Personal Secretary

Place of work: Sickle Cell Centre, Willesden General Hospital

Accountable to: Executive Committee, The Sickle Cell Society

Works for: The Sickle Cell Society

Duties:

1. To type all correspondence as instructed by members of the Executive Committee of the Sickle Cell Society.

2. To type from shorthand and audio dictation.

3. To type the Minutes of the Society meetings prepared by the Secretary, and participate in the preparation of the Annual report.

4. To answer the telephone and take appropriate action.

5. To deal with queries related to the Sickle Cell Society, by telephone or in writing.

6. To keep accurate records of all such queries.

7. To organize and/or supervise sending of publications, i.e. leaflets, reprints etc.

8. To make arrangements for lectures, film shows and discussions as instructed by the Sickle Cell Society.

9. To record all donations to the Sickle Cell Society and submit them to the Society.

10. To undertake such duties that will ensure efficient functioning of the Society and assist in other general work of the Society.

hours to be worked and the salary. This is helpful if the description is being sent out to applicants.

All the examples state to whom the employee is responsible. If this point is not included in the job description then it should be made clear to the prospective employee in some other way – in the contract of employment or the letter offering the job.

If you are only employing one person there is no problem – he or she is responsible to the Executive Committee, or more precisely the chairperson. Being responsible to a Committee of, say, 20 people is not practical: the employee could be given conflicting instructions by different members and be at a loss to know which to follow. If you are employing more than one person it is usual to make one of the appointments the senior employee and for the other staff to be responsible to that person, who in turn will be responsible to the chairperson. In the same way that you want to avoid employees receiving conflicting instructions from different people, so you will also want to avoid the situation where you and other members of the Executive don't know who is doing what or whether anything is being done at all.

Although the last point may appear too formal and inhibiting for the way in which most community groups like to operate, it is easier in the long term to try to prevent friction arising rather than trying to cure it after the problem has arisen. In practice these formalities need not be restrictive or dictatorial. As with almost every aspect of working life, a great deal depends upon relations between individuals and a good measure of common sense. No doubt you will want to encourage your staff to feel they can fully participate in the group's work. It is only sensible, therefore, that if an employee expresses interest and skills in a particular area of work they should be given an opportunity to extend that interest – but only if it is also good for the organisation!

One way of involving staff is to encourage them to attend meetings of the Executive Committee. If you have more staff than is practical for that, then the chairperson and other key members could meet regularly with them. Macclesfield Women's Aid holds a weekly house meeting which is attended by some of the women staying in the Refuge as well as all the staff, the chairperson and another member of the Executive. At these meetings they iron out all the day-to-day matters. In addition, the project manager may attend the monthly meeting of the Executive Committee.

▷What salary should you pay them?

Traditionally, voluntary and community groups have been notoriously bad payers, with the result that they often have difficulty recruiting people of a suitable calibre who will not leave as soon as they find a better paid job. You get what you pay for! This maxim applies as much to the voluntary sector as to industry.

In recent years, however, with the increasing legal, and other, complexities involved in running a community group effectively, and with the growth of temporary employment schemes, the voluntary sector, and its sponsors, have come to realise very few people are in a position to take on a job for love alone and that it is vital to offer the going rate if the job is to be done properly.

Most temporary employment schemes set a maximum on what you can pay; this is negotiated with the relevant trade unions at national level. If, however, you are applying for grant aid from your local authority or a charitable trust or a central government department, you can adopt a nationally recognised salary scale. The ones used by most local voluntary and community groups are the National Joint Council's scales for Local Authority employees, which cover manual, administrative, professional and social work staff. These scales take into account the skills required for the job and the level of responsibility which is entailed. If you decide to use this scale you will find it helpful to contact either the personnel officer at your local authority, or the local representative of the appropriate local authority trade union, or both. They may recommend different starting points on the scale for the same job, in which case it's for you to decide which to follow.

If you prefer to set your own salary level, you will get a good idea of the going rate by looking through the local and national newspapers and comparing those jobs to yours. You will also need to think about how you will deal with pay increases and increments for long-service or extra qualifications.

Groups which choose to use the recognised scales often adopt the terms and conditions of employment which apply to that scale, such as annual holidays, hours of work, and arrangements for sick leave. Again, you may prefer to work out these arrangements for yourself, but it will be necessary to state these in the contract of employment.

- list your reasons for needing staff.
- list all the tasks which need to be done, now and in the future.
- group and prioritise these tasks.
- estimate the weekly time needed to be spent on each task.
- draw up appropriate job descriptions.
- decide upon a suitable level of salary.

▷ Recruiting and interviewing

You can advertise your vacancy

● in local and national newspapers. These are very expensive so keep them brief.

● on local radio. Some local radio stations, particularly in high unemployment areas, have a job-slot for which there is no charge.

● at your local Job Centre. Jobs funded by the MSC have to be advertised at Job Centres. The MSC will do this for you as soon as your application for grant-aid has been approved by them. If you are not taking on staff under an MSC scheme you can just phone in the details yourself.

● through professional recruitment agencies. It is rare for voluntary groups to use these because they charge a high fee to either the employer or the employee or both. Names of agencies will be found in the Yellow Pages under 'Employment Agencies'.

Whatever method of recruitment you use, you will need to give the following information:

● a brief outline of the duties involved.

● the salary, or at least a rough idea.

● any specific qualification or experience that is required.

● the method of application – should they telephone you for an

133

application form, or just write in and enclose a curriculum vitae?

● the closing date and an address to which applications should be sent.

Application forms

Using these ensures you obtain all the information you require to form a clear mental picture of the candidate's qualifications and experience. They make it less easy for applicants to miss out any facts they would prefer you not to know but which could affect your decision to shortlist or appoint them. They also enable an at-a-glance comparison of applicants' abilities.

On the other hand, smaller groups employing only a few people may find the costs of printing application forms prohibitive. Other groups prefer to see what the applicants have to say for themselves, and letters of application are good indicators of candidates' abilities to write clearly – which may be an important aspect of the job.

Drawing up a short-list and arranging interviews

Soon after the closing date for applications has passed you will want to draw up a short-list of candidates to interview. Usually it is only necessary to hold one round of interviews, but if the position is a key one in the organisation, or if you receive so many applications you have difficulty in selecting only a few to interview, you may prefer to hold two rounds of interviews to narrow down the field.

As you go through the applications you should tick off in your mind whether the applicants really meet the level of qualification and experience required for the job. Experienced personnel managers sometimes get hunches about people because over time they have learnt to read between the lines and are able to assess someone's potential more accurately than those less experienced at recruitment. If you don't have such experience, it is better to play safe and look for the obvious signs of suitability in qualifications and years of work experience.

References should be taken up before the interviews are held, if possible. Otherwise any appointment you decide to make should be subject to receipt of satisfactory references, and you should take them up as soon as possible.

A letter should be sent to short-listed candidates at least a week before the interviews are held stating the date, time and place of the interviews. Allow at least half-an-hour for each candidate, longer if the post is a senior one, and ask candidates to contact you if the time is not convenient, or if they decide to withdraw their application.

Before the interview

Inexperienced interviewers are often more nervous than the candidates! As with meetings, careful preparation will help calm your nerves so here are some points you should think about beforehand:

● if several people are doing the interviewing, decide which of you is to lead, or chair, the interviews and whether that person should ask most or all of the questions, or whether you will work round the table each asking a question in turn.

● if you choose the latter, will you each have set questions to ask all the candidates? Or will you ask questions as they occur to you which are appropriate only to the individual candidate?

Your questions should aim to bring out or confirm

● the candidate's qualifications and experience.

● their personal qualities such as good humour, self-confidence, ability to talk fluently and organise their thoughts.

● their interest in the post.

● their attitude towards the work of your organisation.

● what **they** think they can contribute to the job.

● when they are available to start working for you.

In turn, candidates will want to know from you more about their duties, the hours of the job, holidays and so forth. Be sure you can answer these questions.

■ decide how you are going to advertise your vacancy, bearing in mind the type of person you want to apply for the post.

■ are you going to use an application form? If not, list the key points you will be looking for when you read through the letters of application.

■ draw up your short-list and notify these candidates of the interviewing arrangements.

■ take up references.

■ before the interview work out your questions, and be prepared to answer questions from candidates about the job.

Conducting the interview

On the day you should ensure there is someone to welcome candidates as they arrive at your premises and to show them to a waiting room.

● begin by introducing yourself and your colleagues.

● try to put the candidate at ease by asking an easy, conversational question to start with, such as "Perhaps you could begin by outlining your past experience in this field of work", NOT "What makes you think you can do this job?"

● most people find it easier to conduct interviews seated around a table rather than sitting back in low armchairs which can result in paper-rustling, reduce the atmosphere of formality, and may be uncomfortable or embarrassing for the candidates.

● ask open-ended questions, not ones which only require a 'yes' or 'no' answer. Give the candidates time to think about your questions before rushing in to prompt them, and allow them time to answer fully.

● even if you decide after a couple of minutes that this candidate is not for you, be patient and continue with the interview as far as possible so that the candidate feels he or she has been given a fair hearing. Interviews have a public relations aspect and a candidate who feels shabbily treated is unlikely to talk well of your organisation to his or her friends and colleagues.

● after you have asked all your questions, ask the candidate if they have any questions to ask of you.

● finally, thank the candidate for attending; ensure they know how to claim travel expenses, and give a rough idea of how long they can expect to wait before hearing whether or not they have been successful. Don't give any indication of their chances of success at this stage: try to keep an open mind until all the interviews have been carried out.

After the interviews

When all the interviews are over allow plenty of time for discussion amongst yourselves about the merits of the various candidates. It is rare for all the members of an interviewing panel to be unanimously in favour of one particular candidate. It has to be a majority decision and the way in which that decision is reached should be regarded as strictly confidential to the members present. Even if you are not in agreement with the majority it is still your duty as a member of the interviewing panel to give support to the person who is appointed and to help him or her do a good job for your organisation. If there is no clear majority in favour of any of the candidates you can hold another round of interviews of the two or three favourites. If you were not very happy with any of them it is better to advertise again.

Many organisations like to contact the successful candidate by telephone first to confirm they will accept the job, before rejection letters are sent out to the other candidates. A SPECIAL PLEA – **always** send out rejection letters to **all** the unsuccessful candidates including those who never got onto the interview short-list. A common complaint in this time of high unemployment is that employers can't even be bothered to inform applicants that the job has been filled. Not only is this discourteous, it is also hurtful to candidates who may have been unemployed for a long time. It can also be hurtful to your organisation as it will not improve your public image!

Within a day or so of the interview you should write to the successful candidate confirming the appointment and briefly

outlining the main terms and conditions of employment –
salary, hours, holidays, date and place of commencement. Ask
them to confirm in writing as soon as possible that they accept
the appointment on these terms.

- during interviews try to put candidates at
  ease, give them all a fair hearing, and invite
  questions from them.
- after interviews contact the favourite
  candidate before sending out rejection
  letters to other candidates.
- notify **all** unsuccessful candidates.

▷What is a contract of employment?

You are required by law to give appointees a contract of
employment within 13 weeks of their starting. The contract is a
statement of the terms and conditions of employment and,
besides including the items referred to above, should also refer
to any pension scheme, length of notice on either side,
arrangements for sick leave, disciplinary and grievance
procedures and so forth. If the contract is for a fixed term the
expiry date must be stated. There are many books available from
the library about employment but as this is such a sensitive area
of law you should always seek legal advice in drawing up your
contract. The following people will be able to advise you:

● the MSC if you are employing people under a temporary
employment scheme.

● a solicitor – but you will have to pay unless you can find one
who is sympathetic to your group's work.

● your local authority's personnel manager.

● your local CVS or RCC: if they can't help you themselves they
will probably know of a sympathetic solicitor or personnel
manager who will assist you.

● your national or parent organisation's staff.

CONTRACTS OF EMPLOYMENT ACT 1972

STATEMENT OF CONDITIONS OF SERVICE

Name.............................
Date of commencement of employment: Date on which this statement issued:

1. You are employed in the service of Macclesfield Women's Aid and you are appointed to the post of...

2. Duties will be carried out at such place of employment in the Macclesfield Area as may be required by the Management Committee. The actual working base being the Refuge.

3. Confirmation of your appointment will be subject to satisfactory completion of a probationary period you will be expected to establish your suitability for the post.

4. You are employed on a week to week basis, subject to a maximum of 52 weeks or less, if the scheme is terminated by the Manpower Services Commision or the employer.

5. **Hours:**
   i)   Your working week is of   hours.
   ii) Your working hours are flexible to meet the contingencies of the Project.
   iii) Time off in lieu may be authorised at the discretion of
   iv) We would expect staff to be available to attend meeting, including evening meet-
        when necessary, for which time off in lieu is allowed.

6. **Salary:**
   i) Your current salary is £   p per week gross.
   ii) You will be paid weekly by cheque.

7. **Travel:**
   An allowance of '   p per mile or public transport rate can be made for approved Project business, subject to budget limits. This allowance does not include travel between home and the normal place of work.

8. **Sickness allowance and statutory sick pay:**
   You are allowed.................sick leave with full pay and............on half pay.
   Sickness benifit will be deducted from salaries. A certificate of sickness will be required after more than 3 days consecutive absence. A Doctor's certificate or statement will be required after 7 days consecutive absence or in the event of frequent recurrent absence.
   Statutory Sick Pay is paid for the first eight weeks, by the employer, for any absence due to sickness — no payment will be made for absence of 3 working days or less.
   Details of the Statutory Sick Pay Scheme may be obtained from your local DHSS Office or the Management Committee.

9. **Leave:**
   Your annual leave entitlement is............days for each completed month of full-time employment. Holidays should be taken during the project and not after this is ended. Statutory and Bank Holidays may also be taken. Leave dates should be notified in advance and approved by the Project Manager.

10. **Notice:**
    The minimum period of notice to which you are entitled under the Act is one week.
    The minimum period of notice you are required to give is not less than one week.

11. **Pension:**
    There is no pension scheme.

12. **Outside Interests:**
    The Women's Aid Committee will allow reasonable time off for employment to:
    a) Carry out Trade Union duties and activities.
    b) Perform Public Duties.
    c) Attend interviews for permanent employment.

13. **Disciplinary and Grievance Procedures:**
    The procedures to be followed are set out in the document attatched to this statement.

14. **Other Conditions:**
    The statutory rights of employees are set out in documents available through the employer.

15. **Agreement:**
    All parties accept that this agreement can be reviewed in the light of experience.

16. **Social Security Pensions:**
    A contracting-out certificate under the Social Security Pensions Act 1975 is/is not in force for the employment in respect of which this written statement is issued.

17. **CONFIDENTIALITY**
    Because of the nature of the work you are employed to do it is of vital importance that the location of the refuge or the identity of its residents is not disclosed to unauthorised persons. Any breach of confidentiality could result in disciplinary action.

Other legal aspects on which you should seek advice, or become familiar with are:

● **The Health and Safety at Work Act 1974**, and its related fire precaution and safety legislation.

● **Employers' Liability (Compulsory Insurance) Act.** This requires employers to insure against their liability for bodily injury or disease sustained by employees.

● **Employment Act 1980 and Employment Protection (Consolidation) Act 1973** which cover contracts of employment, trade union activities, maternity rights, rights to a minimum period of notice, unfair dismissal, and redundancy payments.

Leaflets about employer's duties and all of the above Acts are available from local Job Centres.

Getting into training

Hull Community Work Training Group, which was set up with representatives from three community associations, the local Volunteer Bureau, Council for Voluntary Service, Education Association and Hull Federation of Community Associations, has successfully applied to the Manpower Services Commission for funds for a part time Community Work Training Officer, under the Voluntary Projects Programme.

The Group was formed in September 1982 to promote training opportunities for volunteers and paid workers involved in voluntary organisations and neighbourhood groups. The Training Officer will take a special interest in the needs of unemployed volunteers and community associations.
Is this an idea worth copying? Further information is available from Jan Brooker, Neighbourhood Worker, 3 Eastgate, Hessle, North Humberside HU13 9NA.

from "Community" Spring 1983

▷ Is staff training necessary?

Schemes funded by the MSC require the employer to arrange for staff to receive adequate training for the job and, in the case of young people, to be allowed to attend college for one day a week for further education.

Whether or not you are required to provide training for your employees, it is always a good idea to do so: it enables your

MACCLESFIELD WOMENS AID   DECEMBER 1983

Staff Training

Now that the refuge is operating and underway, thanks to the terrific practical effort put in by the team, we felt it would be an idea to offer some training concerned with other less tangible aspects of the job.

We have compiled a training package, the aims of which can be seen as follows:-

1.   To give staff an insight into the kind of women likely to need the refuge, their environment, lifestyle and other problems they are likely to bring with them.

2.   To confirm the philosophy of Women's Aid; how other refuges operate on this philosophy; how it is applied to our refuge and a 'firm up' on policy.

3.   To give staff an opportunity to consider their own personal and professional development in their job, what experience they hope to gain, what role they feel they have in the team, what problems, if any, they wish to resolve etc.

We hope the training arranged will be enjoyable and useful to you in your work at the refuge and will enable us to run an efficient and caring refuge for battered women - our mutual aim.

staff to talk to staff from other groups to exchange ideas and discuss activities for your group. Staff often return from a one-or-two day course able to take a new look at their employing organisation, and it gives them confidence to tackle old problems in new ways. Conferences are another way of providing training as most conferences organised by voluntary organisations include discussion sessions and workshops.

■ draw up a Contract of Employment and give this to your employee within 13 weeks of the date on which they commence work.

■ obtain adequate Employers' Liability insurance.

■ work out a staff training programme.

▷Temporary employment schemes

In theory all voluntary groups are vulnerable to annual reviews of their grants by the government department which has awarded these to them. Some groups, however, have succeeded in negotiating with their local authority or relevant national government department which recognises the longer term funding importance of their work. For most groups, though, funding is only temporary and this is particularly so for schemes funded by the MSC some of which are only permitted to last one year. The following is an outline of the main types of grant aid, all of which have an expiry date.

The community programme

This is an MSC scheme for unemployed adults and funding of salaries and overheads lasts for 52 weeks only. Frequently this means no sooner have you got someone trained and experienced in the job than you lose them and, if continuation of funding is approved by the MSC, you have to take on a different unemployed person. Your choice for the job is also limited as you can only choose from amongst people who have been registered with the Job Centre for a year, or six months if the person is aged 18 to 24 years.

The youth training scheme

This now incorporates all the previous MSC schemes for young unemployed people, such as Youth Opportunities, Work Experience Programme, Work Experience on Employers' Premises and so on. For approximately 8 young people you provide places

---

Good talker

Lighthall Youth and Community Association in Solihull have successfully applied to the Manpower Services Commission for money for an interviewer. The interviewer will conduct a survey of local needs and generate involvement in 'Layca'.

Recruiting drive

£6,000 has been given by the DHSS Opportunities for Volunteering Fund to Longsight CA in Manchester. The grant is for a full-time community transport driver who will recruit volunteer drivers.

both items from "Community" Summer 1983

for on a youth training scheme, you are able to employ one unemployed adult. Becoming a sponsor of a youth training scheme is a lengthy business, and very complex. Again, funding is only for one year which means you get an annual changeover of young people and most of your adult staff.

Urban Aid

Most grants made under the Urban Aid scheme last for five years but the government expects the local authority to pick up the whole of the tab after that. In recent years local authority expenditure cutbacks have caused considerable problems for voluntary groups whose urban aid has expired. They have been faced with making redundancies and closing shop.

Voluntary projects programme

The aim of this programme is to promote adult education and community activity for the unemployed. Paying volunteer organisers is permitted, as is some capital expenditure on premises, but again funding only lasts for one year. It also allows for out-of-pocket expenses of up to £5 to be paid to volunteers without prejudicing their entitlement to unemployment benefit or social security.

Opportunities for volunteering

Again, projects are limited to one year. The aim of this scheme is to provide opportunities for unemployed people to help other people in need, such as the elderly, physically and mentally handicapped, victims of crime and isolated mothers of young children. The grant covers salaries of project organisers, volunteers' expenses and the cost of training, for organisers and volunteers.

None of these schemes permits voluntary groups to plan and develop their work because of the temporary nature of the grants. They do, however, enable a group to get started, show it can make a valid contribution to the community and hopefully go on to negotiate long-term arrangements for grant aid from their local authority.

10 A HOME OF YOUR OWN

▷ Why do you need premises?
▷ Temporary premises
▷ A permanent home of your own?
▷ Construction or conversion?
▷ What will a building cost?
▷ Planning legislation
▷ Furnishing and equipment
▷ A travelling home

KNOW YOUR WELFARE RIGHTS !!

LONDON TRANSPORT

EVERYONE
WELCOME ➤

▷Why do you need premises?

Finding suitable premises was a major challenge for three of the five community groups whose stories start this book. Both the Macclesfield Women's Aid and the Earlstown Opportunity Groups soon found that their premises were too small. Feltham Community Association managed for two years without a building of their own and had to campaign hard and vigorously to get a semi-derelict school.

In all three cases, obtaining premises was an integral part of these groups' aims. Womens' Aid groups' main reason for existence is to provide accommodation for battered women; a community association is limited in the events it can mount without its own building.

In addition to these practical reasons for wanting to find premises, most groups want a place of their own in order to give them an identity, to hold meetings, receive phone calls and mail, and be available to the public.

Before rushing out to scour the town for the ideal home for your group, you should seriously consider:

● is it really necessary for you to have premises?

● will they be worth the costs and work involved? Would the money consumed by rent, rates, heating etc. be better spent on providing other services to your members or the public, such as information leaflets or a newsletter? Would your members' time be better spent on these things rather than trying to maintain an office which is rarely used? Would it be cheaper and simpler to hire rooms as and when they are required?

● what exactly will you do with an office or house or shop? **Make a list of all the activities for which premises, other than your own homes or other free premises, are essential.** How often are you likely to hold these activities each year and what are the charges for local halls or meeting rooms? Compare these to the costs of running your own premises all day and every day of the year.

If you decide premises are vital to your work then read on . . . . If not, then consider yourself lucky – the hassle involved in occasionally having to book halls or squash around small dining tables in members' homes is nothing compared to the headaches involved in running premises!

What will you use your building for?

Think about the type of activities you intend to organise:

● how often will these happen?

● which activities can share rooms?

● how important is storage space?

● how important is location in terms of bus routes and the population who will use the premises?

● how much outdoor space do you need for car parking, play area, and so on?

● can disabled people get in and about the building?

Getting down to details, it's not too early to think about **room layout.** The main point to make here is avoid wasted space – rooms that are hardly ever used; wide corridors leading nowhere; areas that can't be used because of inadequate light or heat.

One thing community groups often underestimate is the need for storage space. If you are regularly going to hire out some of your rooms to other community groups you will need to give them ample space for keeping their equipment. Ideally each room should have some storage space within or adjacent to it. Remember: the Earlstown Opportunity Group had to remove its equipment each day!

There are strict standards about the number of lavatories to be provided in a building for use by the public: your local planning officer will give you these details. If you provide kitchen facilities you should ensure that these are adequate to your needs and those of other users of the centre and that they will meet the approval of your local Environmental Health Officer, located at your district council, who will advise you on the laws about catering and hygiene.

Most planning departments require that new buildings be accessible to disabled people before they will grant planning permission; they can also make this a requirement when converting buildings. RALAR (the Royal Association for Disablement and Resettlement) can advise you on good standards for disabled persons' access; you can contact them at 25 Mortimer Street, London W1N 8AB.

■ list the activities for which you need a building.

■ how many rooms, and roughly what size, will you need for these activities?

■ how often will you need to use those rooms?

■ can you manage with less space by sharing?

■ where should your premises be located?

■ have you allowed for plenty of storage space?

■ have you got a sufficient number of toilets? Do you need access to a kitchen?

■ is the building accessible to disabled people?

When you have a clear idea of what you want you can start to look around.

▷ Temporary premises

Initially, you may have to make do with temporary premises which can become permanent if they prove suitable. If permanency is essential from the start, as with a community centre, you may have to make do with local halls as and when required, like Feltham Community Association, whilst you go through the lengthy business of obtaining grant-aid from your local authority, followed by planning permission and, eventually, construction of the centre.

If you decide to obtain temporary premises you should start by considering the following options:

● **your local CVS or RCC** may have rooms available for regular hire, or they may agree to act as a **poste restante** for letters and pass on your address to callers. The Sickle Cell Society were given a room at Brent Community Health Council for their base.

● **local churches and premises of other community groups**

148

such as community centres may be able to loan you a room on a regular basis. FCA offer most of their rooms to other voluntary groups.

● **empty shops and offices** – the local authority will be able to tell you who is the owner of these, that is, who is responsible for paying rates. Other sources of information are estate agents and neighbouring shops and offices who may be willing to give you the address of their landlord.

● **spare rooms or parts of public buildings,** such as schools due to be demolished sometime in the future: contact your local authority to find out which government department presently owns these. Premises in areas affected by road proposals are usually owned by the Dept. of Transport and you may be able to get them to agree to a short let as Macclesfield Womens' Aid did. Other buildings owned by central government departments, and presumably left empty because the work for which they were built is no longer carried out there. Such old tax or DHSS offices are usually managed by the Dept. of Environment's Property Services Agency. Addresses of local offices of these departments will be in your telephone yellow pages. You have to be prepared to be very nosey and persistent in your enquiries about empty buildings owned by public authorities! You will be amazed at the reasons they can present for not letting you use them, even for only a few months.

Building a play space

Tygre CA, in the Essex village of North Weald, have their very own wasteland scheme. It involves the transformation of a piece of land called, accurately, the Field into a community resource. The council has promised the land, local business will provide cultivation expertise. All that now remains is for the residents to get along and enjoy their new recreation ground.

from 'Community' Summer 1982

149

● **empty houses on council estates:** contact your local housing department about these. If nothing else, you should expect from them a valid reason why the house is empty and must remain empty.

Some points to bear in mind if you find temporary premises:

● **are the costs worth it** or would you be better saving your donated cash and grants for your permanent home?

● **what type of lease are you taking on?** If it is for a fixed term will you be able to negotiate an extension of time and, if so, is your rent subject to review? Also, what length of notice is required if you decide to give up the premises? Is this length of notice reasonable? On the other hand, is your landlord required to give you reasonable notice? Finally, beware all-repairing leases: you may take on a dilapidated shop and find yourself responsible for fully restoring it. Usually the landlord is responsible for external and structural repairs whilst you will be expected to maintain the inside. Before signing any lease go through the property and list the faults within the interior and give a copy of this list to the landlord, so that you can avoid being accused of not having maintained the premises to the standard in which it is claimed they were originally leased to you.

● **location of the premises.** This applies to permanent premises as well and will be discussed in more detail later on, but you will want to consider again whether being inaccessible to the people you want to reach is not worse than having no premises at all for the first six months or so.

● **will your temporary premises affect the image you want to give to the public and prospective members?** If you have no control over the decor and furnishings and are stuck with some dingy cupboard, you may feel it is better to wait until you have a place people will want to visit and in which your members can take pride.

● **do you have enough people at this early stage to run the office/shop/centre for all the time you intend to be open?** Or would you be better waiting a while until you can get a grant from either your local authority or the MSC for employment of workers to run a regular and reliable service? Nothing is more annoying than going out of one's way to find a group's office only to find them closed at the times they advertise to be open. It's a recipe for losing members and public support.

▷A permanent home of your own?

There are many reasons for groups to want their own premises. Existing accommodation in the area may be inadequate, expensive and over-booked. Many districts don't have church halls, adult education centres and the like for hire by voluntary groups and finding a home of your own is the only option.

You should begin your search for permanent premises by contacting your local authority to ensure there are no proposals in the pipeline which might duplicate your premises. You should find out whether there are any other voluntary groups in your area who are also thinking of acquiring their own premises, and with whom you might share the headaches.

▷Construction or conversion?

Nowadays suitable sites for new buildings are at a premium in urban areas and community groups have had to give greater attention to converting old buildings. This has resulted in some exciting and imaginative projects like the conversion of an old bath house into a community centre, use of old churches for youth workshops and so on.

Grand site for a centre

Highcliffe C.A. in Dorset are hoping to convert a grand house into their new community centre. "Greystones", an Edwardian gentleman's residence which in its time has been a barracks, a nursing home, flats for the elderly and a derelict but listed building, should prove to be one of the most distinguished community centres in England when work is completed. A list of their activities reveals the need for a large scale centre. Sections include bridge, catering, choir, community art, dress making, French, frets and strings, German, keep fit, mens forum, music, yoga, wine making, travel club, rambling, theatre and junior.

from 'Community' Spring 1982

151

Converting a building is often as expensive as constructing a new one, but it does have advantages. An old building will already have an identity and character of its own in the neighbourhood which may attract help from those who knew it in its former state of glory. It is far easier to attract support – physical and financial – for a building which already exists than for one which is only on paper. And you may be able to attract additional grant aid under various environmental schemes. There are some problems though, and before deciding upon any particular building you should work out your precise requirements.

Having said all that, what often happens is that a member spots an empty building, the group decides it will do and only then does it start to work out its actual requirements. This may work well, but beware of taking on a building larger than you really need as this could turn out to be very costly in heating and maintenance, or a building which is inadequate for your purposes and on which you may spend a lot of money for very little return.

Using existing buildings may also present legal difficulties. For example, many old buildings have restrictive covenants upon them, which means that the person who originally donated the school or church to the community stipulated that certain activities should not be permitted on the premises. The most common restriction is the sale of alcohol, and would limit a building's use as a community centre or other place for social occasions. Some old buildings are 'listed' as having historical or architectural interest; acquisition of these may involve you in a great deal of expense as the exterior may have to be restored and maintained to their original standard. They may not be suitable for your needs even though the extra grant-aid from your local authority may meet most of the extra costs.

If you decide to go for a new building you will need to give thought to many of the questions about suitability, raised above, as well as the type of construction you want, although this may be decided for you by the local planning department. Where a new building is desirable or necessary, you have a choice between 'system-built' – prefabricated – or traditional methods of construction. System-building is quicker and usually cheaper but offers less flexibility in planning the room layout. On the other hand traditional methods may reduce repair and maintenance difficulties as local tradesmen will be more familiar with them. They are also more attractive and can blend in with

Three phases of a success story

Caversham
Park
Community
Centre
opened
in
January
1977

Caversham Park Village
Association, Reading,
Berkshire.

by John F. Grimes

Caversham Park is a 'new'
village, the building of
which was completed some ten
years ago. Set on the
northern outskirts of
Reading, it consists of some
1500 houses, bungalows and
flats. Although all the
planned residential units
were completed, the
'Community Centre for the
social benefit of residents'
promised in the original
plans was never started by
the developers.

In 1965, shortly after the
first houses in the village
were occupied, half a dozen
or so like-minded residents
got together. They dis-
cussed what might be done to
enable the rapidly growing
number of new villagers to
enjoy a full and varied
social life, and decided
that an association should
be formed " ... to establish
and manage a Community
Centre where people may meet
to follow social pursuits."

From the very beginning the
members of the Association
aimed high. They decided
that only the best would be
good enough for the village.
The site where the planned
centre should have stood was
still available and so they
set to work. Many hours of
work were put into fund
raising events, planning and
designing the new building
and making contacts with
organisations that might
loan cash for the project.

First phase

It was decided from the out-
set to plan the centre so
that construction work could
be carried out in stages,
allowing one 'phase' to
become operational while
cash was being raised for
the next. The first phase
was to include a coffee
lounge, meeting room, kitchen, toilets and a bar.

Eventually, impressed by the
enthusiasm of the association
(and possibly by the substantial amount of money they
had already raised) the
local authorities agreed to
loan them the necessary
cash so that construction
work could start. Tenders
were submitted and the first
bricks were laid.

It was indeed a proud moment
for all concerned when in
January 1977, nearly twelve
years after the formation of
the association, the first
phase of the Centre was
opened by the Rt. Hon. Sir
Harold Wilson. It was a
tremendous achievement and
no one could have faulted
the association had they
left it at that. But they
had not been idle during the
months when Phase I was
being built. More plans
had been made and more funds
raised; enough in fact to
finance the building of two
squash courts as an addition
to the complex. These were
completed and ready for use
by early 1979.

The association was now
gaining momentum. It was
already a recognised Com-
munity Association and a
registered charity. It was
(and still is) publishing
its own monthly magazine
called 'Village Voice' to
keep villagers informed of
current news and affairs of
local interest. More and
more of the village population were joining its ranks
and it had been possible to
form several groups to cater
for special interests.
These groups cover a whole
range of pastimes from
amateur dramatics to sub-
aqua, badminton to ballet.

The association's next project, Phase II of the complex, was a Youth and
Recreation Wing. The
'Village Festival Week',
which by this time had
become an annual event, and
other fund-raising activities
helped raise the money. In
mid-1981 the builders moved
in and by early 1982 the
building was completed. A
great feeling of pride and
achievement was felt when on
24th June 1982 His Royal
Highness the Duke of
Gloucester peformed the
official opening ceremony.

Today the association is
busy planning further projects including the addition
of two more squash courts to
the complex. At the same
time it continues to promote
a real feeling of community
amongst the residents of the
village.

All this has been achieved
entirely through the voluntary work of its members and
residents of the village.

from 'Community' Autumn 1983.

the surrounding buildings. And they may prove cheaper in the long run as they are more durable. For example, investment in a sloping roof could save you cash and time spent on dealing with excess water collection on a flat roof.

Whether you decide to go for conversion or construction you should first seek professional advice from an architect. Their fees are high but if you go through with the project and succeed in getting a grant they can be included in the estimates. On the other hand if you do not want to take the initial risk, you will be able to get free and expert advice from the voluntary organisation NUBS (Neighbourhood Use of Buildings and Space) at Inter-Action, Tel. 01-267 9421. NUBS is a group of professional volunteers, architects and surveyors who will give you some advice free of charge and a full architectural service at a reduced charge. The Royal Institute of British Architects at 66 Portland Place, London W.1. may also be able to put you in touch with an architect who will advise community groups at reduced rates.

▷What will a building cost?

Before you get involved in payments to architects, contact with planning departments and so forth, you should work out what you can afford.

Many people who have ever had anything to do with starting community groups become obsessed with finance. So often the money side is overlooked whilst imaginations run riot and the result can be a white elephant. However good your ideas for your premises, you have to keep your feet firmly on the ground. Acquiring a building will probably be the most expensive and difficult task your group ever has to face, so at each stage you should ask yourself: is this or that item really necessary? Can its cost be justified in terms of use to your members?

Begin by working out how much the type of premises you need will cost to run. This is called **current expenditure** (or operating costs) and it will include:

● maintenance, repairs and re-decoration

● replacement of furniture and equipment

● heat and light

● telephone, postage and stationery

- rates – you can claim a reduction in local rates – see Chapter 6, but not water rates

- cleaning and caretaking

- insurance

- security – you may need a burglar alarm if you are storing expensive equipment on the premises, or it may be required by the insurance company against vandalism and theft

- licence fees

- interest charges and repayment of any loans you have had to take out to pay for the construction/conversion work

Against these costs you should now compare your income – and be honest about your income! Local groups may tell you they will use a room in your building when it is at the planning stage, but change their minds later on. Perhaps they will have their own premises by the time yours is built. Also, beware of putting charges so high that no one can afford to use your building.

It is a good idea to think of alternatives to fall back on if it turns out your income is not as high as anticipated. For example, what would a local caterer pay you for regular hire of your main room for weddings or parties? They have the advantage of usually taking care of all cleaning and caretaking for these occasions which saves you more money. What will the local authority pay you to use a large room for a youth centre, or day centre for the elderly?

More is said in Chapter 6 about budgeting.

You should obtain estimates for capital costs of building or converting the premises from several builders. Your local authority's officers are not permitted to recommend any particular builder so you have to look around for the best deal yourself. Look carefully at any absurdly low tenders – it is not worth trying to cut costs by going to disreputable builders because if they don't do the work to standard it is **your** building which will be pulled down if it doesn't pass the building control inspection. This is where an architect's services are particularly helpful as he or she will know whether the materials quoted by the builder are adequate for the job.

There are several schemes for giving grants to community groups for capital expenditure. The most popular is the Urban

Aid Scheme under which your local authority pays 25% and the Department of Environment 75%. This scheme has been affected by cuts in public expenditure however, and competition for these funds is fierce. Inner city areas cannot claim Urban Aid but instead can apply to their local authority for funding under the Inner City and Programme schemes.

Grants to cover all or most of your capital expenditure will be based on the estimates you submit when making your application. If it turns out the building costs more than you estimated you will not be given the extra; if it turns out to be less your grant will be reduced accordingly. This is another reason why it is not worth trying to cut corners when you obtain tenders from local builders.

Details of how to apply for the above and other grants are contained in Chapter 7.

If your application for a capital grant is refused you will be faced with either abandoning the project or raising the money from other sources, usually fund-raising or by a private bank loan. The latter is very expensive as it attracts high interest rates and should be avoided if at all possible. On the other hand fund-raising can often be slow and painful whilst building costs are rising all the time, and in any case £100,000 is an awful lot of money to raise, although it has been done.

If your first application for a grant is refused it is worth asking your local councillor and officers at the Town Hall if they would give you a reduced amount, say 75% of the amount you need, if you promise to raise 25%. Some local authorities are very tight with their grants and instead prefer to make low interest or interest-free loans. Although these are preferable to bank loans, you should think hard before you take on any loan. You will be committing yourself and future members of the group to many years of hard work before they can actually claim the building belongs to the group.

We're on the right scent

Meanwhile Gardens Community Association together with the local branch of MIND have set up a community enterprise project. A team of 8 paid workers and a supervisor are to build a scented garden to give pleasure to the neighbourhood in general and the visually handicapped in particular. They also hope to start a furniture repair workshop employing 7 people under the community enterprise programme.

from 'Community' Winter 1981

156

- work out your annual running costs for the building.

- work out your annual income from the building and compare these to the costs.

- is there a shortfall? If so, how will you meet this?

- obtain at least three tenders from reputable builders, and compare these looking for differences in quality of materials used, guarantees which will be given, time factors etc.

- can you get a grant from your local authority to cover the whole or part of the cost?

- if not, can you get a cheap or interest-free loan? Will your income enable you to keep up repayments?

Heat and light

After salaries and building repairs, the largest item of expenditure for most groups with their own premises is heat and light. Electric heating systems are usually considered cheaper to install but cost more to run, whilst gas is expensive to install but cheaper to run. Points to consider in keeping your heating costs to a minimum are whether the heating can be properly controlled by thermostats and whether it can be turned off in rooms left empty for long periods. Also think about **who** will control the heating – casual users adjusting a thermostat located in a room or by the senior employee in charge of the building? If possible, it is worth including double glazing and other forms of insulation in your estimates for construction of the building.

▷ Planning legislation

Planning permission is not about whether a building is structurally sound but whether it will fit into the community. It applies to new buildings and to changes of use of existing buildings. If you do not know whether you need planning permission, ask the planning department at your district council. They will give you the necessary forms and advice on how to present your application. The decision is not up to the staff of the council, however, but the elected members of the planning committee.

Use of an existing building will probably require 'change of use' permission, even though there may be no building work involved; for example, you just want to use a house as it stands for an office. Applications for change of use are considered as full planning applications (see below). If the building is 'listed' you must obtain 'listed building consent' if there are to be any changes made to the outside.

Where you do intend carrying out building work, either on a new or converted structure, you will need to get full planning permission.

There are two methods for obtaining this:

● you can first obtain outline planning permission which means the local authority approves in principle the work you intend to carry out. For this you will have to prepare drawings in sufficient detail to show the size and form of development. You can do these yourself, or you may be lucky enough to have a member of the group with experience in technical drawing. After receiving outline planning permission you will need to submit detailed plans in order to obtain approval of reserved matters. This means your detailed plans must comply with any reservations made by the local authority about your outline plans, such as location of access to the building, style, height and so on.

● you can go straight away for full planning permission which requires you to submit the detailed plans. Although detailed plans are normally drawn up by an architect, they do not have to be and you could use your technical drawings instead.

Anyone can make an application for planning permission but they must inform the owners of the land that they are doing so. Beware of agents or vendors offering you land on which they have been unable to obtain planning permission at a price which they raise after you have obtained planning permission. Your solicitor can negotiate an 'Option to Purchase' with the agent or vendor's solicitor to prevent this situation arising.

A fee is charged by the planning department for each

application. For Outline Planning Permission this is approximately £60 for each 1000 square metres of site. Your local planning officer will give you details of these charges.

- check whether you will need 'Change of Use' permission.

- are you going to head straight for Full Planning Permission, or start with Outline Planning Permission, followed by Approval of Reserved Matters?

- have you informed the owners of the land or building?

Building Regulations

Nearly all building work requires approval under Building Regulations whether or not planning permission is required. This includes buildings for which only 'Change of Use' permission has been given. Building Regulations ensure buildings are constructed to the required standard of health and safety.

When you apply for full planning permission you will have to submit three copies of the detailed plans to your local council's building control department. Copies of the Building Regulations are kept at most public libraries, but as they change frequently you should ensure the copy you use is up to date.

From the date of receiving your plans the building control department has up to five weeks to inform you of their decision. If you receive no answer in this time, you can assume approval of the plans. The work has to be carried out within three years of the date of their approval. As the work progresses, your builder will have to send cards into the department informing them that various stages of building have been completed. A building inspector will then come and inspect the work. If it is not up to standard, they have the authority to tell the builder to do the necessary work.

Again, there is a fee for obtaining Building Regulation approval. This is on a sliding scale according to the value of the building and you should consult your local building inspector about it.

Safety precautions

Any building for use by the public, new or converted, will have to meet the approval of the fire department. They will pay particular attention to access to emergency exits, adequate provision and positioning of fire-fighting equipment, placing of fire doors, and a fail-safe system of emergency lighting. They will also state maximum numbers, seated or dancing, permitted in the main rooms, if you have any large enough for such functions.

While your building is still at the drawing-board stage, it is advisable to talk to your local fire prevention officer about these safety requirements as they may have a bearing on your room layout and building costs.

A building used by the public will require a fire certificate and your local fire prevention officer will also be able to tell you how to obtain this.

Under the **Health & Safety at Work Act**, employers of more than four employees are responsible for ensuring the health, safety and welfare of their employees. You are also liable for ensuring the safety of members of the public who use your building. If you are in any doubt about the safety of your

£84,000 Community Centre scheme set to go ahead

Building at Bow Baths, by Audrey Shilling

In November 1980 local residents set out to secure the redundant slipper baths in Bow, East London, which had been standing empty for five years, as a Community Centre. They began to raise money to put the building in order and convert it for use by people of all ages.

Funds have now been secured to go ahead with the scheme. The £70,000 has come from the GLC, London Borough of Tower

Hamlets, City Parochial Foundation, Tudor Trust, Coopers Company and others. A further £14,000 is still needed to complete the scheme, and the result of an application through the Government's Urban Aid Programme is expected shortly.

When completed the Centre will provide a social club and games room, a hall and changing rooms, two meeting rooms, a room for use by advice groups, and a resources room equipped with typing and copying facilities.

from 'Community' Summer 1983

premises, you can ask your local Health & Safety Officer at your district council to inspect the premises and advise you about how they may be improved if necessary. This is particularly relevant if you are using an old building which may have hazards of which you may be unaware.

Adequate insurance is also vital, not only for the structure and contents of the building but also against accidents to employees and the public. NCVO publishes a useful leaflet about insurance for community groups called **Insurance Protection for Voluntary Organisations and Voluntary Workers**, price 65p inclusive, available from Macdonald and Evans Distribution Services Ltd, Estover Road, Plymouth PL6 7PZ. Some national, umbrella organisations have arranged insurance schemes at reasonable rates for their local branches.

Licensed premises

If you want a room with a licensed bar for your own members or for hire to the public, you will need to obtain a licence for the sale of alcohol. Licensing laws are complicated but NFCO has produced an excellent book called **Bars, Charity and the Law**. You may be able to persuade your local library to get it for you.

You may require licences for other activities as well, such as performance rights, music and dancing, film shows, lotteries and so forth. An outline to the legal position on these and other licensing regulations is set out in NFCO's leaflet **Licensing and Other Statutory Requirements for Community Associations and Village Halls**.

■ did you remember to apply for approval under the building regulations when you applied for Full Planning Permission?

■ contact your local fire officer, and also your local Health and Safety Officer.

■ have you got adequate insurance for the building, contents, employees, **and** the people who will use it?

■ do you need to obtain any licences for sale of alcohol, filmshows etc.

▷Furnishing and equipment

If you are lucky enough to receive a grant for your building, you may be able to afford a good standard of furniture which will add to the welcoming image of your centre. But if you are having to raise the funds from donations, good furniture will probably be low on your priority list. It should not be so low, however, that no one comes to the centre more than once because it is so dingy and uncomfortable. In many ways the interior is more important than the outside and there are ways you can make your rooms bright and attractive without paying a great deal.

If you have a local MSC Youth Workshop in your area they may be able to renovate and build furniture for just the cost of materials – and you may be able to beg these from public appeals, furniture stores, your local education department and so on. You can acquire paint and curtain materials by similar means. Decent carpets are harder to come by, so only use these in rooms for which they are essential.

It is always worth shopping around, particularly for office equipment where firms are falling over themselves to sell to you. Never refuse donations of old office equipment – you can always use it in part exchange for something better!

Plants and pictures give the finishing touches to making a place friendly: local nurseries or market traders may be willing to give you the plant cuttings they haven't been able to sell at their best, and bright posters can often be obtained from local cinemas, travel agents and record shops.

A useful person to get to know is your county council's purchasing officer who may allow you to purchase goods from them at their reduced prices, or place orders with companies on your behalf which will save you paying VAT.

Another way to brighten up your centre is to find someone to do some murals for you – on outside and/or inside walls. Feltham Community Association were lucky to have amongst their membership an artist, Peter Howson, who decorated the main hall, and another member who painted the murals in the licensed bar and childrens' room.

▷A travelling home

Some community groups use a vehicle as their base. Double

decker buses are particularly popular with Welfare Rights groups who want to be able to hold advice sessions in different neighbourhoods, and playgroups who use them as Playbuses. Toy and equipment libraries are other examples of mobile community groups.

Many community groups, such as the Earlstown Opportunity Group, are dependent on having regular access to reliable transport. Sometimes it is possible to share the cost of buying and running a vehicle with other groups in your area, or your local authority may be able to arrange for you to use one of their school minibuses, or day-centre ambulances. It is worth asking around before committing yourself to buying your own bus. Or you may be lucky enough to get one donated – some voluntary groups have been very successful in applying to the car manufacturers.

If you acquire a vehicle, don't forget:

● to get it taxed.

● to get adequate insurance for drivers and passengers.

● if it is over one year old and has eight or more seats, you must get an annual test certificate.

11 THE WAY FORWARD

▷ Preparing for the Annual General Meeting
▷ Reviewing your group's progress
▷ What went wrong, and what you can do about it
▷ Change and growth of your group
▷ Community planning

ABC COMMUNITY GROUP
COMPUTERISED RECORDS

THE WAY FORWARD

▷ Preparing for your Annual General Meeting

Every registered charity, limited company or industrial provident society has to hold an Annual General Meeting at which it presents a report to its members about the group's activities during the preceding year.

Although there are certain formalities which have to be carried out at the meeting, AGMs need not be boring or awe-inspiring events. Many groups use them as a chance for members to meet each other by following the business part of the meeting with a social event. This encourages members to attend the meeting and may bring additional benefits through publicity and raising of funds.

Be sure to allow yourself plenty of time for preparation. Although the main responsibility for arrangements rests with the secretary and the chairman, this is an event in which all members of the Executive should be encouraged to participate.

Notice of the meeting

Opposite is a typical agenda for an AGM. Notice that it is much simpler with fewer items than an agenda for an Executive meeting.

Your constitution will set down the minimum period of notice required for the AGM. If nominations for officers and Executive members are needed **before** the meeting, you will have to send out nomination papers with the agenda and stipulate a date by which these must be returned, and to whom.

If there are more nominations than available positions, you will have to arrange for a vote to be taken at the meeting. This may be by a simple show of hands or require a secret ballot. It is the job of the secretary to ensure all contingencies are taken into account.

The Annual Accounts

Chapter 6 explains how these should be set out. Frequently the accounts are included in the Annual Report. When presenting them to the AGM the Treasurer will need to give a verbal report summarising the group's financial position and drawing attention to any significant changes for good or bad which have occurred during the year.

The chairperson, secretary and treasurer must be prepared

SOULSBURY COMMUNITY ASSOCIATION

Annual General Meeting
to be held on

21st November, 1983
8.00p.m.

at the Soulsbury Community Centre.

(1) Apologies for Absence

(2) Minutes of the last Annual General Meeting
held 19th Nov. 1982

(3) Presentation of the Annual Report

(4) Presentation of the Annual Accounts

(5) Election of Officers:

> Chairperson
> Vice-Chairperson
> Treasurer
> Secretary

(6) Election of the Executive Committee
(12 members)

(7) Appointment of Bankers and Auditors

(8) Any other matters relevant to the Annual General
Meeting

This meeting will be followed at 9.00 - 11.00p.m.
by a hot-pot supper and disco to raise funds
for the Centre. Tickets £1. from the Secretary.

to answer questions, and sometimes criticisms, from members about their reports.

The Annual Report

It is not essential for you to publish a lengthy report. Items which have to be included are:

● names of officers.

● names of other trustees or directors (Executive members)

● names of members of other committees, sub-committees etc.

● a summary of the group's activities during the past year.

Some groups like to use their annual report as publicity material containing far more information than is legally necessary, and presenting it in an attractive, readable style with cartoons and illustrations. This type of report can be useful for fund-raising. You can include a copy with your letters of application as it gives potential donors a complete picture of your group's work.

After the AGM

The secretary will need to take minutes of what happens at the meeting. To save postage these are usually circulated with the following year's agenda for the AGM. But within a month of the AGM, copies of those minutes and details of new trustees and directors, together with the Annual Report and Accounts, must be sent to the Charity Commission and/or the Registrar of Companies.

■ allow plenty of time to prepare for your AGM.

■ send out agendas and nomination papers in accordance with your constitution.

■ make your Annual Report readable and attractive.

■ be prepared to answer questions on the Report and Accounts.

■ take minutes of the AGM and send these with your Report, Accounts, and details of new trustees to the Charity Commission and/or Registrar of Companies.

▷Reviewing your group's progress

Why do you need to monitor your progress?

● your funding agency will probably require a statement of your progress before they will decide whether to give you a grant for a further year.

● it is good practice to assess your work: there is always a danger that the group will become cosy and complacent, forgetting its original aims and why you all felt they were important.

One of the main features of the voluntary sector has been its ability to change and develop according to the needs of the community. It is this capacity for flexibility which has made it pioneer of many ventures taken up by the welfare state at a later, safer stage. Careful monitoring of your work will enable you to look ahead and to participate in the progress of your community.

How do you monitor the group's progress?

● by collecting statistics.

● by carrying out forms of research to obtain people's views and opinions.

Basically, you have to think about the best ways of comparing your actual achievements against your desired achievements. You may find it helpful to go back and read those sections of Chapter 3 which deal with research methods.

Collecting statistics

To do this you will first need to establish a suitable method for keeping records and to think about what information you will need to enable you to quantify your achievements.

The records you keep should be as simple and unambiguous as possible. They must be easily understood by the person with the task of maintaining and collating the information. It is advisable to make one person, either staff or a volunteer, responsible for maintaining records so the work is done consistently.

For example, Macclesfield Women's Aid are under some pressure to prove the need for their existence to the District

Council in order to get a larger house. With the help of a volunteer research student they have designed a simple form, shown on the next page, which is completed for every woman who contacts them. The form provides staff at the Refuge with essential personal details – names, numbers of children – and will also be useful for obtaining precise figures on the need for a Refuge in the town, their contact with welfare services and so on.

Sorting through this type of information can be a chore, particularly if you have a large number of records. An organisation which may be able to help you with this type of record-keeping is your local Information Technology Centre (ITeC). There are currently some 150 ITeCs being opened around the country. Their main aim is to provide training in electronics, computing and modern office techniques to school leavers under the Youth Training Scheme. But ITeCs will also do work for local businesses and community organisations as part of their trainees' practical experience. Usually they make only a small charge to cover overheads incurred by these services, which include:–

● word-processing: useful for printing of newsletters, updating of directories; fund-raising mailshots; large numbers of minutes and agendas.

● computer bureau services: for example, your accounts, monthly financial statements and forecasts; PAYE; employee and volunteer records; collation of survey information.

● adult education and training: introductory courses in computing, word-processing.

● information services: via Prestel, Viewdata.

Most ITeCs will help you design the records you need to keep and will also update and collate these for you when required. You need not worry about confidentiality – if you like you can give each client or volunteer a number, and only you need hold the list of names and corresponding numbers.

Alternatively one of your members may have a home computer on which you could keep your records. Again, your local ITeC will be able to advise you on how to use it for this purpose.

Although some community groups are doubtful about the use of computers in their work, they can take a lot of the drudgery

Macclesfield Women's Aid.
objective . . . to provide a refuge for battered women and children

Referred by:..date...............

Worker/s involved...

<u>RECORD FORM</u>

Name...

Address..

....

<u>Children:</u>

Name.............................age.......school..............

Name.............................age.......school..............

Name.............................age.......school..............

Name.............................age.......school..............

Name.............................age.......school.

Name.............................age.......school..............

Date accommodated.....................

Date of leaving..................... (actual length of stay......)

D.H.S.S. letter issued...............

<u>Service provided:</u>

Accommodation ☐   Welfare Rights Information ☐

Housing Advice ☐   Legal advice ☐

other ☐   please specify...

<u>Referred to other services:</u>

Police ☐   Marriage Guidance ☐   Probation ☐

Social Services ☐   Education Dept. ☐   Housing Dept. ☐

Solicitor ☐   other ☐   please specify...................

<u>Outcome of intervention:</u>

Returned home to husband/cohab.   ☐
Returned home husband/cohab. moved out ☐
Moved out of area   ☐
Re-housed   ☐
Other   ☐   please specify...

171

out of record-keeping as well as enabling you to get more out of those records, leaving you with extra time to concentrate on the more important aspects of your work.

HANDICAPPED children from the Earlestown Opportunity playgroup were given a surprise on Monday when they received several remote-controlled cars from trainees of the St Helens Information Technology Centre.

The cars which cost about £15, had been bought for a few pence and repaired by trainees as part of their work experience at ITEC.

Mrs Caroline Pinder, deputy manager of ITEC, said: "A group of trainees in our electronics department repaired the cars as part of their training, and were so pleased with the finished

Trainees put playgroup on right road . . .

result they decided to give them to a children's group.

"As they are so easy to operate, we thought they would be particularly useful to handicapped children."

ITEC are now appealing to other shops in the North West who may have similar toys in need of repair.

Mrs Pinder said: "We would very much like toy shops with any old, faulty cars

to contact us so we can repair and distribute them to other handicapped children at Christmas."

ITEC which was set up in September, runs a 50-place Youth Training Scheme in which young people can get experience in computing, electronics and modern office techniques.

Besides repairing toy cars, trainees also hope to under-

take other practical projects such as repairing cassette recorders and radios for blind people, as well as providing business and computing services for industry.

The remote-controlled cars were presented to the playgroup by trainees Karen McWilliams, of Collingwood Road, Newton, and Adrian Owen, of Elephant Lane Thatto Heath at St John's Church Hall, Earlestown.

The playgroup, which was set up by St Helens Handicapped Children's Trust, is in need of more strong, sturdy toys and would be grateful to anyone who could provide some.

from 'St Helens Reporter' October 1983

The Sickle Cell Society have raised the money to acquire a micro-computer on which they keep details of all their 850 or so members. This saves them hours of time spent typing addresses for sending out their newsletters, as well as checking on membership subscriptions and putting new members in contact with others living in their part of the country.

Carrying out other forms of research

Of course, some of the information you need for your progress review will not be so easily quantified. Perhaps you will want to know about the effects on your members of reduced hospital services or rising unemployment in the area; or their views on your group's activities and what changes they would like made. These broad questions will have a bearing on how you decide the group should develop in the future but they are less easy to measure.

A popular way is to do a survey, either full or sample, on the lines of that set out in Chapter 3. Again, refer to other sources such as local and national government reports and the findings of other community groups which give weight to your arguments. It will make your research much more readable if you include quotes from users of the project and also your volunteers.

- establish a simple record-keeping system.
- make one person responsible for maintaining your records.
- periodically collate the information contained in your records.
- obtain views and opinions by doing a survey.
- refer to sources of national and local statistics.

▷What went wrong, and what you can do about it

Perhaps your research will indicate you have not achieved your objectives. For example, your attempts to persuade the local authority to reduce the number of empty council houses in the area have failed. Why?

Amongst the aspects you will have to consider will be your

tactics. Was your publicity wrong? Were there not enough of you to carry out all the campaign work? Did you fail to work out a proper campaign of action? Did you underestimate your costs? And so....

Again, all these questions provoke the question Why? And you will have to look hard at both the organisation and yourselves to see where you went wrong. Were you too busy arguing amongst yourselves, or too busy socialising with each other? Or was there never enough time at meetings to discuss the most important items because the evening was taken up with trivia?

To answer these sorts of questions you will have to go back to square one, reviewing your objectives and the way the group is organised. Perhaps your meetings are too informal, or the absence of a treasurer has meant the finances are in a mess, or your internal arguments have lost you valuable new members, or you have too many chiefs and not enough injuns! You are going to have to face up to these problems and tackle them or they may jeopardise the future of the group. Sometimes it is better to start all over again, trying to get it right the second time around, like Macclesfield Women's Aid.

▷Change and growth of your group

On the other hand, perhaps the reason you failed to achieve your objectives was because of circumstances beyond your control. For example, you may have obtained considerable sympathy and commitment from your local authority to reduce the number of empty properties, but a change in the Rent Act or taxation laws has led to more private landlords finding it beneficial to leave properties empty, or the recession has made it harder to sell houses in the area.

Alongside these developments there may have been an increase in the numbers of young people being thrown out of home, or families made homeless when they can't keep up rent payments following redundancy of the main bread-winner.

In the light of these developments, your group may feel it would be more appropriate to broaden or even change your objectives and to take on additional work. You could, for example, start a housing co-operative to provide homeless people with temporary homes in some of the vacant properties.

Of course, such a decision will have considerable impact upon your existing organisation and resources in terms of money, premises, volunteers and so on. You will need to consider how realistic it is for you to take on this extra work and, whether in doing so, you won't lose sight of your original aims which were to pressure **others** to make better use of the empty houses. You may decide it is more appropriate to continue with your original aims but give a new slant to your campaigning work to take in these new developments.

If the social problem you've uncovered requires immediate and practical attention which you don't feel your group can give, you could approach your local CVS and other voluntary groups in the area about taking on such a task, rather than taking on something to which you're not entirely committed and which might cause dissension within the group.

▷ Community planning

As an established community organisation you can expect to be consulted in your district and county council's future plans for your community. This may include housing and transport developments, environmental schemes, education and health facilities, town planning and so forth.

Unfortunately, not all local councils are diligent about seeking the views of local groups even though your members will ultimately be the consumers of these plans and therefore have a right to be asked about issues which will affect their lives.

If your council fails to contact you for your views, you have to do your own research by reading the planning notices in local newspapers, attending local planning committee meetings and exhibitions. Always make your views known in writing.

Kirkstall Village CA of Leeds (Spotlit in COMMUNITY last year) have had a major success. They have won their fight to prevent the local Electricity Board put a massive string of pylons through Morris Wood, a local beauty spot. Celebrating the victory, the Yorkshire Evening Post said that not only has the Association cultivated a new sense of community belonging but can and does retain treasured features of the local environment. The Association's triumph was the result of intensive voluntary effort at a week-long Public Inquiry. Congratulations Kirkstall!

from 'Community' Winter 1981

175

If your bus service is cut or a local shop closes

What can you do to stop the rot?

COMMUNITY PLANNING - GETTING INVOLVED IN ENVIRONMENTAL CHANGE

By Liz Hurst, Streetwork

We are all planners. We all make decisions which affect our future lives, we all think about our prospects and opportunities. Yet much of the environmental planning process is outside our control. We can still be affected by decisions made by someone else without reference to our needs or wishes. And sometimes this can be a painful experience. When a local factory closes, or a housing estate is badly designed or falls into disrepair, or the local bus service is cut or the corner shop closes down, the effects can be immediate and devastating, but what can a local community do?

Community Response

Increasingly, the response of many community groups has been to take action themselves. Sometimes groups choose to lobby their local politicians, but others have sought a more direct approach. It's seldom an easy path to tread, but the achievements of groups like the Weller Street Housing Co-op in Liverpool, or the Lewisham Self-Build Housing Association in London - both of whom have designed, built and managed their own new homes - shows that communities CAN plan their own surroundings and should be given more opportunities to do so.

Sources of Help

The problems of getting involved can be very great indeed. Vested interests, bureaucratic inertia, professional jealousy and a simple lack of time and expertise amongst groups can all combine to make an already difficult process even more so. But sources of help do exist, and a variety of aid agencies have sprung up around the country committed to increasing community access to environmental decision making and to encouraging self help.

Planning Aid and Community Technical Aid

The Town and Country Planning Association (TCPA) has a national network of volunteer planners who will help local groups. It also runs a special GLC funded, service for London which is complemented by the Planning Aid for Londoners scheme run by the Royal Town Planning Institute (RTPI) - these groups pass cases between themselves according to who can best

help with the problem.

TCPA also runs a Community Technical Aid Centre (CTAC) from its Manchester Office, which provides a comprehensive grant-seeking and design service for local groups. Similar agencies also exist elsewhere, notably COMTECHSA in Liverpool and the Newcastle Architectural Workshop - TCPA is currently compiling a list of them all.

Community Education and Local Studies

Another way of dealing with environmental issues is through community education. The Urban and Local Studies movement encourages children and adults to study their own surroundings, to analyse the problems and to participate in change as part of a local working network of understanding and action. Work in Notting Dale Urban Studies Centre in West London shows what a powerful force this could be. To give one example, children studying the problems faced by elderly residents in a large tower block showed the results of their research to an embryonic tenants groups on the estate. Old people were an invisible problem - other tenants had no idea that so many were trapped in their flats, unable to get to the shops or the pub, and were horrified. After much work, the result was a new community centre on the estate - designed, built and run by the tenants themselves. STREETWORK, the Unit for Urban and Local Studies, work across the country to promote this approach to school and community education by offering held and advice, running workshops, helping to set up Urban Studies Centres, publishing reports and producing monthly the Bulletin of Environmental Education.

Addresses

TCPA, 17 Carlton House Terrace, London, SW1Y 5AS (Tel 01 930 8903)

STREETWORK, Notting Dale USC, 189 Freston Road, London, W10 6TH (Tel 01 968 5440)

CTAC, 61 Bloom Street, Manchester M1 3LZ (061 236 5195)

RTPI, 26 Portland Place, London, W1N 4BE

COMTECHSA, Westminster Chambers, 3 Crosshall Street, Liverpool, L1 6DQ (051 227 2204)

Newcastle Architectural Workshop, 6 Higham Place, Newcastle upon Tyne, NE1 8AF (0632 328 183)

from 'Community' Summer 83

If you feel the interests of people living in the community have been ignored you may want to consider appealing to the Department of Environment's planning inspectors, or going to your local Ombudsman.

Local Ombudsmen investigate complaints from the public about injustice caused by maladministration in local government. You can obtain a brochure about their work and a complaint form from your local Citizens Advice Bureau. There is also a Parliamentary Commissioner, or national Ombudsman, to investigate complaints of injustice which occur because of central governmental maladministration. Complaints to him can only be referred by your Member of Parliament, so he or she is the first person you have to see. However, you can make a direct approach to the Parliamentary Commissioner if your complaint is about the National Health Service, but your complaint must be in writing and within one year of the matter occurring.

- ask – and answer – yourself honestly "What went wrong?" and "What went right?" and WHY?

- is it practical for your group to take on additional work?

- is there another group more suitably placed to take on that new work?

- try to get involved in planning matters. How will changes and new developments affect your members?

- make your views known in writing.

There are many places and people from whom you can get advice and practical help in starting your community group. This chapter is a quick-reference guide to these resources and covers:

● **local places and people to visit for advice and assistance**

● **useful books and contacts listed under chapter headings**

● **addresses and phone numbers of useful national organisations**

● **addresses of government departments and agencies**

● **who does what in local government**

▷ Local places and people to contact for advice

Your local community worker

Contact him or her through your local Social Services, Education or Leisure Department. They will help you to get your group started and tell you whether any similar projects already exist in your area.

Local Authorities

A table showing the functions of district and county councils is on page 192. Most councils have an Information Department where you can call in, with or without an appointment, to look at the various statistics kept by them – the number of people on the local housing waiting list; the number of local firms employing more than 50 people. You can also ask to see past copies of council and committee minutes, although the minutes of some sub-committees may not be available to you. Particularly useful sources of information are the District and County Structure Plans, and the background or technical reports on which these are based. These contain historical figures as well as forecasts for changes in a community's population structure, employment prospects, housing needs, and so forth.

Councils for Voluntary Service (CVSs) and Rural Community Councils (RCCs)

These are voluntary organisations whose job is to co-ordinate and promote voluntary activity in their locality. CVSs operate in urban districts and RCCs cover the rural areas of shire counties. They will be able to tell you whether a group with aims similar to yours already exists in the area. If you're not part of a group yet, they may know of other individuals in the area faced with the same difficulties and be able to put you in contact so you can work together to start a self-help group. Frequently they employ Community Development Workers who will be able to give you practical advice and assistance in starting your group. Again, their telephone number will be in your telephone directory or available from your local library.

Community Associations

These are voluntary organisations operating in a clearly defined neighbourhood or part of a town. Many of them have a Community Centre. Like CVSs and RCCs they will be able to tell you what facilities already exist in your neighbourhood as well as giving you assistance to get started.

Community Health Councils

Our health service is a very complex machine, and the best people to advise you on where to obtain information – if they haven't already got it to hand for you – is your local Community Health Council. CHCs are the consumer-watchdogs for the health service. They are an invaluable source of hard facts about all aspects of health provision as well as reviews of the standards of health care in their locality and details of proposals for future services. The address of your local CHC will be in your telephone directory or on the noticeboard in your local library.

Local Public Libraries

All of the items kept at your local council's information Department are also available at your local library. You may prefer to go there rather than the council's offices as you will have longer to browse through the reports. Public libraries also keep a very wide range of other useful reference books in particular the **Directory of British Associations** which is a list of non-statutory organisations in the UK. It gives addresses and telephone numbers for a wide range of voluntary groups from bee-keepers' clubs to national welfare agencies and professional associations. Back copies of local and most national newspapers are also kept at libraries and if you can't find what you want, the librarian will order a copy for you. Amongst the most useful reference books available at most public libraries are **the latest available editions of:**

The Municipal Year Book
The Hospital, Social Service and Education Yearbooks
The Charities Digest 1983
The Sunday Times Self-Help Directory
The Conservation Source Book
Directory of British Associations
Councils Committees and Boards
Annual Abstract of Statistics
Monthly Digest of Statistics
Economic Trends
Census 1981 County Reports (produced for every County in the U.K.)

▷Some useful books and contacts
(Listed by Chapter Headings)

Chapter 3 – Getting Started

BOOKS: (if address of publisher is not given below please see Contact List).

'The Community Group's Handbooks' Set of five short books 65p each or £2.70 the set, including post and packing, from the Community Projects Foundation.

'Consumers Guide to local government' from the National Consumer Council.

'Guide to Social Services' from the Family Welfare Association.

'Directory of Voluntary Organisations' from the National Council for Voluntary Organisations.

'The Investigator's Handbook' from Community Action, 27 Clerkenwell Close, London EC1 (price 40p).

'Citizens Advice Notes' (a legal compendium, with regular updates, payment by annual subscription) from the National Council for Voluntary Organisations.

'Manual for Action' from the Action Resources Group, c/o 13 Mornington Grove, London E3 4NS, price £2.50.

'Sources of Social and Legal Information' from P. Byrne, Penzance Branch Library, Morrab Road, Penzance. Price £1.20 (inc. p & p), send cash with order.

CONTACTS: (Please see General Section of Contact List on page 187)

Chapter 4 – Getting Organised

BOOKS: (if address of publisher is not given below please see Contact List)

'Charitable Status – A Practical Handbook' by A. Phillips and K. Smith, from Inter-Action Inprint, £3.95.

'The Charity Commissioners: How they can help Charity Trustees' a free booklet from the Charity Commission.

'Constitutions Workpack' from the Scottish Council of Social Services, price £1.50.

'How to set up a Neighbourhood Co-op' from the Co-Operative Development Agency.

CONTACTS:

Charities Aid Foundation, 48 Pembury Road, Tonbridge, Kent TN9 2JD (Tel. 0732-356323).

Charity Trading Advisory Group, 9 Mansfield Place, London NW3.

Charity Commission for England and Wales:
  Southern Office – 14 Ryder Street, St. James's, London SW1Y 6AH (Tel. 01-214 6000).
  Northern Office – Graeme House, Derby Square, Liverpool L2 7SB (Tel. 051-227 3191).
  Central Register – St. Alban's House, 57-60 Haymarket, London SW1Y 4QX (Tel. 01-214 6000).

Registrar of Companies, Companies House, Maindy, Cardiff (Tel. 0222-38858).

Inland Revenue Claims Department
  England, Wales & Northern Ireland: Magdalen House, Stanley Precinct, Bootle, Lancs. L69 9BB.
  Scotland: Trinity Park House, South Trinity Road, Edinburgh EH5 3SD.

National Co-Operative Development Agency, 20 Albert Embankment, London SE1 7TJ.

Registry of Friendly Societies, 17 North Audley Street, London W1Y 2AP (Tel. 01-629 7001).

Chapter 5 – Making Meetings Work

BOOKS: (if address of publisher is not given below please see Contact List)

'Working on a Committee' by S. Clarke from the Community Projects Foundation (£1.00 inc. p & p).

'The Club Secretary's Guide' by H. Quinn, published by David & Charles, price £3.95 (order through an ordinary bookseller).

'Citrine's ABC of Chairmanship' from 11 Dartmouth Street, London SW1, price £3.25 (inc. p & p).

'A Guide to Effective Meetings' from The Industrial Society, 3 Carlton House Terrace, SW1Y 5DG, price £1.95 (inc. p & p).

'Hours into Minutes – a guide to minute taking' from the British Association for Commercial and Industrial Education, 16 Park Crescent, London W1, price £2.25 (inc. p & p).

CONTACTS: (Please see the General Section of the Contact List for organisations providing training for honorary officers.)

Chapter 6 – Looking After the Money

BOOKS: (if address of publisher is not given below please see Contact List)

'How to manage your money, if you have any' from the Community Accountancy Project, £1.50, 34 Dalston Lane, E8 8AZ.

'A Guide to the Benefits of Charitable Status' by Michael Norton from the Directory of Social Change.

'Bars, Charities and the Law', £4.50 to members of NFCO (£9.00 to non-members).

'Covenants – a practical guide to the tax advantages of giving' by Michael Norton, £4.45 from the Directory of Social Change.

CONTACTS: (please also see those listed in the General Section of the Contact List on page 187.)

Charities Information Bureau, 161 Corporation Street, Birmingham B4 6PT (Tel. 021-236 1264).

Social Service Supplies, Stepfield, Witham, Essex CM8 3BY (Tel. 0245-380465).

Charities Aid Foundation, 48 Pembury Road, Tonbridge, Kent TN9 2JD (Tel. Tonbridge 356323).

Legislation-Monitoring Service for Charities, St. John's College, Oxford OX1 3JP (Tel. Oxford 47671 ext. 244).

Chapter 7 – Getting the Money

BOOKS: (if address of publisher is not given below please see the Contact List)

'Raising money from Industry'
'Raising money from Government'
'Raising money through Special Events'
'Raising Money from Trusts'
£3.20 each

'A Guide to Company Giving', £8.95.

'Raising Money for Capital Projects: Fund Raising Notes', £2.95.

'Leaving Money to Charity', £1.95.

'Marketing: A Guide for Charities', £4.95.

'Charity Christmas Cards', £3.95.

'Legacies: A Practical Guide for Charities', £3.95.

'Raising Money Through Advertising', £3.95.

'A Basic PR Guide', £2.50.

'How to be a Good Trustee', £3.95.

'Investment of Charity Funds', £1.95.

all from the Directory of Social Change

'Sources of Statutory Money', £1.25 from NCVO.

'Directory of Grant-Making Trusts' from the Charities Aid Foundation at £20 (but available in most public libraries).

'Lotteries and Gaming – Voluntary Organisations and the Law', 65p from NCVO.

'Fund-raising: a guide to the Literature', £1.50 from NCVO.

CONTACTS: (please also see the Contact List on page 187.)

Charities Aid Foundation, 48 Pembury Road, Tonbridge, Kent TN9 2JD (Tel. Tonbridge 356323).

Special Programmes Division, Manpower Services Commission, Selkirk House, 166 High Holborn, London WC1 (for information see Appendix 2)

Charities Information Bureau, 161 Corporation Street, Birmingham B4 6PT (Tel. 021-236 1264).

Chapter 8 – Publicity

BOOKS: (if address of publisher is not given below please see the Contact List)

'Using the Media' by Dennis McShane, from Inter-Action Inprint, £3.00.

'The Community Newspaper Kit' from Inter-Action Inprint, £1.95.

'Print – How you can do it yourself' by J. Zeitlyn, Inter-Action Inprint, £2.30.

'List of Print-Making, Photography, Film and Video Facilities', £1.00 from Artic Products, 17 Shakespeare Terrace, Sunderland.

'Making News' by Barbara Lowndes from National Federation of Community Organisations, £2.50.

'How to get the Message Over' by Dilys Lewis from National Federation of Community Organisations, £1.50.

'The Local Radio Kit' by Keith Yeomans and John Callaghan from the National Extension College, 18 Brooklands Avenue, Cambridge. Book and cassettes for £5.95.

'Media Project News' from the Media Project, Volunteer Centre, Berkhamstead by annual subscription.

'Directory of Media Training Opportunities' from Community Service Volunteers, £1.15.

'See 4' quarterly journal from Channel 4 Television.

'Directory of Social Action Programmes' quarterly journal from the Media Project at the Volunteer Centre.

CONTACTS: (Please also see General Section of the Contact List on page 187.)

Fantasy Factory, 42 Theobalds Road, London WC1 Tel. 01-405 6862 (offers advice about video and film facilities).

National Federation of Community Organisations (has a range of publicity material for Community Associations including car stickers, badges, poster blanks etc.).

IBA, 70 Brompton Road, London SW3 1EY Tel. 01-584 7011.

BBC (Radio and Television Headquarters), Broadcasting House, London W1A 1AA.

Channel 4 Education Liaison Officer, Channel 4 Television, 60 Charlotte Street, London W1P 2AX.

Chapter 9 – Recruiting Staff and Volunteers

BOOKS: (if address of publisher is not given below please see the Contact List)

'Who Takes the Strain? The Choices for Staff Support' from the National Youth Bureau.

'Job Evaluation Kit' £1.00 (inc. p & p) from Voluntary Action Westminster, 1 St. Mary's Terrace, London W2 1SU.

CONTACTS: for addresses of organisations which provide training for staff and volunteers please see the General Section of the Contact List on page 187. These organisations also give advice about employment legislation, salary levels etc.

Chapter 10 – A Home of Your Own

BOOKS: (If address of publisher is not given below please see Contact List)

'Insurance Protection for Voluntary Organisations and Voluntary Workers' £2.50 from the National Council for Voluntary Organisations.

'Bars, Charities and the Law' – £9.00 (£4.50 for members) from the National Federation of Community Organisations who also produce a useful series of information sheets about running a Community Centre.

'Waking up Dormant Land' from CoEnCo, Zoological Gardens, Regents Park, London NW1, price £3.40 (inc. p & p).

CONTACTS: (please also see the Contact List on page 188.)

Neighbourhood Use of Buildings, c/o Inter-Action Trust.

Royal Institute of British Architects, 66 Portland Place, London W1.

Town & County Planning Association, 17 Carlton House Terrace, London SW1 (Tel. 01-930 8903).

Chapter 11 – The Way Forward

BOOKS: (if address of publisher is not given below please see the Contact List)

'Consumer's Guide to Local Government' from the National Consumer Council.

'Voluntary Sector and Local Authority Collaboration on Environmental Improvement' by J. Bishop, from S.A.U.S. University of Bristol, Clifton, Bristol, £3.30.

'Monitoring Voluntary Action', £2.25 from ARVAC, 26 Queens Road, Wivenhoe, Essex.

'The Activists Dilemma: Local Government Decision Making and How to Influence it' from Thamesdown Voluntary Service Council, 47-48 Fleet Street, Swindon, Wilts. Price 75p.

'Your Right to Attend Planning Committee Meetings' from the Town and Country Planning Association. Price 10p.

CONTACTS: (please also see the General Section of the Contact List below)

Local Information Technology Centres – obtain the address of your nearest ITeC from your local Council for Voluntary Service or MSC Area Office (for the address of your local area office please see the list of Central Government Depts. on page 191).

Community for Local Administration in England, 21 Queen Anne's Gate, SW1H 9BU (Tel. 01-930 3333).

Commission for Local Administration in Wales, Derwen House, Court Road, Bridgend, Mid-Glamorgan CF31 1BN (Tel. Bridgend 61325).

Planning Aid Service, c/o the Town and Country Planning Association, 17 Carlton Terrace, SW1Y 5AS.

Community Computing Network, 83a Mansfield Road, Nottingham.

New Technology Group, NCVO, 26 Bedford Square, London WC1.

Contact List – National Organisations which give information and advice

GENERAL: (These organisations can give advice and assistance to community groups on all aspects contained in this book)

Action Resource Centre, Henrietta House, 9 Henrietta Place, London W1M 9AG (Tel. 01-629 3826).

Association of Community Workers, Colombo Sports and Community Centre, Colombo Street, Blackfriars, London SE1 8DP (Tel. 01-633 0628).

Community Projects Foundation, 60 Highbury Grove, London N5 2AG (Tel. 01-226 5375).

Community Service Volunteers, 237 Pentonville Road, London N1 6NJ (Tel. 01-278 6601).

Directory of Social Change, 9 Mansfield Place, London NW3.

Inter-Action Advisory Service (also Inter-Action Trust and Inter-Action Inprint), 15 Wilkin Street, London NW5 3NX (Tel. 01-267 9421).

London Voluntary Service Council, 68 Chalton Street, London NW1 (Tel. 01-388 0241).

National Consumer Council, 18 Queen Anne's Gate, London, SW1H 9AA (Tel. 01-222 9501).

N.C.V.O. (National Council for Voluntary Organisations), 26 Bedford Square, London WC1B 3HU (Tel. 01-636 4066).

N.F.C.O. (National Federation of Community Organisations), 8-9 Upper Street, London N1 0PQ (Tel. 01-226 0189).

Scottish Council of Social Service, 18/19 Claremont Crescent, Edinburgh EH7 4HX (Tel. 031-556 3882).

Trades Union Congress (to obtain the address of your local Trades Council), Congress House, Great Russell Street, London WC1B 3LS. (Tel. 01-636 4036).

Volunteer Centre, 29-33 Lower King's Road, Berkhamstead, Herts. (Tel. 044-27 73311).

SPECIALIST ADVICE (also refer to lists at end of each chapter)

Housing

Shelter, National Campaign for the Homeless, 157 Waterloo Road, London SE1 8UU (Tel. 01-633 9377).

National Federation of Housing Associations, 30-32 Southampton Street, London WC2E 7HE (Tel. 01-240 2771).

National Tenants Organisation, 7 Galba Court, Augustus Close, Brentford, Middx. (Tel. 01-568 5415).

Town Planning

Town and Country Planning Association, 17 Carlton House Terrace, London SW1Y 5AW (Tel. 01-930 8903/4/5).

Services to Community Action and Tenants, 31 Clerkenwell Close, London EC1R 0AT (Tel. 01-253 3627).

Civic Trust, 17 Carlton House Terrace, London SW1Y 5AW (Tel. 01-930 0914).

Families

Child Poverty Action Group, 1 Macklin Street, London WC2B 5NH (Tel. 01-242 3225/9149).

National Council for One Parent Families, 255 Kentish Town Road, London NW5 2LX (Tel. 01-267 1361).

Family Welfare Association, 501-505 Kingsland Road, Dalston, London E8 4AJ.

Family Service Units, 207 Old Marylebone Road, London NW1 5QP (Tel. 01-402 5175).

Children and Young People

Fair Play for Children, 248 Kentish Town Road, London NW5 2AB (Tel. 01-485 0809).

National Playing Fields Association, 25 Ovington Square, London SW3 1LQ (Tel. 01-584 6445).

Pre-School Playgroups Association, Alford House, Aveline Street, London SE11 5DH (Tel. 01-582 8871).

National Youth Bureau, 17-23 Albion Street, Leicester LE1 6GD (Tel. 0533-554775).

National Children's Home, 85 Highbury Park, London N5 1UD (Tel. 01-226 2033).

Playboard, Association for Children's Play and Recreation (Tel. 021-233 3399).

Women's Issues

National Women's Aid Federation, 374 Gray's Inn Road, London WC1 (Tel. 01-837 9316).

Women's Research & Resource Centre, 190 Upper Street, London N1 1RQ (Tel. 01-359 5773).

Disabled people

The Disabled Living Foundation, 346 Kensington High Street, London W14 8NS (Tel. 01-602 2491).

Disablement Income Group, Attlee House, 28 Commercial Street, London E1 6LR (Tel. 01-247 2128).

Disability Alliance, 1 Cambridge Terrace, London NW1 4JL (Tel. 01-935 4992).

RADAR (The Royal Association for Disability and Rehabilitation) 25 Mortimer Street, London W1N 8AB (Tel. 01-637 5400).

Invalid Children's Aid Association, 126 Buckingham Palace Road, London SW1W 9SB (Tel. 01-730 9891).

Elderly people

Age Concern, Bernard Sunley House, 60 Pitcairn Road, Mitcham, Surrey CR4 3LL (Tel. 01-640 5431).

Help the Aged, 32 Dover Street, London W1A 2AP (Tel. 01-449 0972).

National Federation of Old Age Pensions Associations, Melling House, 91 Preston New Road, Blackburn, Lancs. (Tel. Blackburn 52606).

The Pre-Retirement Association, 19 Undine Street, London SW17 8PP (Tel. 01-767 3225).

Health

Association of Community Health Councils for England & Wales, 362 Euston Road, London NW1 (Tel. 01-388 4943).

British Pregnancy Advisory Service, Austy Manor, Wootton Wawen, Solihull, West Midlands B95 6DA (Tel. Henley-in-Arden 3225).

Standing Conference on Drug Abuse (SCODA), 3 Blackburn Road, London NW6 1XA (Tel. 01-328 6556).

National Council on Alcoholism, 3 Grosvenor Crescent, London SW1X 7EE (Tel. 01-235 4183).

MIND (The National Association for Mental Health) 22 Harley Street, London W1N 2ED (Tel. 01-637 0741).

MENCAP (Royal Society for Mentally Handicapped Children and Adults), 123 Golden Lane, London EC1Y 0RT (Tel. 01-253 9433).

After-care of offenders

NACRO (National Association for the Care and Re-settlement of Offenders) 169 Clapham Road, London SW9 0PU (Tel. 01-582 6500).

National Association of Probation Officers, 1st floor, Ambassador House, Brigstock Road, Thornton Heath, Surrey, CR4 7JG (Tel. 01-689 1116).

Unemployment

National Unemployment Action Association, 318 Summer Lane, Newtown, Birmingham B19 6RL (Tel. 021-359 6596).

Co-operative Development Agency, 20 Albert Embankment, London SE1 7TJ.

Trades Union Congress (for details of local Trades Councils and unemployment centres), Congress House, Great Russell Street, London WC1B 3LS (Tel. 01-636 4036).

Foundation for Alternatives, The Rookery, Addenbury, Near Banbury, Oxfordshire (Tel. 0295-810993).

Council for Small Industries in Rural Areas (CoSIRA), 141 Castle Street, Salisbury, Wiltshire SP1 3TP (Tel. 0722-6255).

Centre for Employment Initiatives, 140A Gloucester Mansions, Cambridge Circus, London WC2H 8PA (Tel: 01-240 8901).

Ethnic groups

Joint Council for the Welfare of Immigrants, 44 Theobalds Road, London WC1X 8SP (Tel. 01-405 5527).

Commission for Racial Equality, Elliott House, 10-12 Allington Street, London SW1E 5EH (Tel. 01-828 7022).

AFFOR, 1 Finch Road, Lozells, Birmingham B19 1HS.

Environmental Issues

Friends of the Earth, 377 City Road, London EC1V 1NA (Tel. 01-837 0731).

Greenpeace, 36 Graham Street, London N1 (Tel. 01-251 3020).

Shell Better Britain Campaign, c/o Nature Conservancy Council, P.O. Box No. 6, Huntingdon, Cambs. PE18 6BU (Tel. 0480 56191).
Provides a comprehensive, free information pack which includes names and addresses of environmental organisations.

British Trust for Conservation Volunteers, 36 St. Mary's Street, Wallingford, Oxfordshire OX10 0EU (Tel. 0491 39766).

Legal Issues

National Council for Civil Liberties, 21 Tabard Street, London SE1 4LA (Tel. 01-403 3888).

Legal Action Group, 28a Highgate Road, London NW5 1NS (Tel. 01-485 1189).

Central Government Departments and Agencies

Approaching central government departments is usually more complicated than visiting your local council offices. The telephone Yellow Pages is a good place to start, or another visit to your public library to glance through 'The Municipal Yearbook' which lists the addresses of all national and regional departments, boards and committees. Then it's a question of try and try again until you obtain the information you want.

I. Addresses of Main Government Departments

Voluntary Services Unit, The Home Office, 50 Queen Anne's Gate, London SW1H 9AT (Tel. 01-213 7079).

Department of Health and Social Security, Alexander Fleming House, Elephant and Castle, London SE1 (Tel. 01-407 5522).

Department of Education and Science, Elizabeth House, York Road, London SE1 (Tel. 01-928 9222).

Department of the Environment, Becket House, 1 Lambeth Road, London SE1 (Tel. 01-211 7992).

Department of Employment, Caxton House, Tothill Street, London SW1 (Tel. 01-213 3829).

Manpower Services Commission, Selkirk House, 166 High Holborn, London WC1 (Tel. 01-836 1213).

II. Addresses of Government Agencies

Arts Council of Great Britain, 105 Piccadilly, London W1V 0AU.

Countryside Commission, John Dower House, Crescent Place, Cheltenham, Gloucester GL50 3RA (for Wales: 8 Broad Street, Newtown, Powys SY16 2UU).

Sports Council, 70 Brompton Road, London SW3 1EX.

Commission for Racial Equality, Elliott House, 10-12 Allington Street, London SW1E 5EH.

Equal Opportunities, Overseas House, Quay Street, Manchester M3 3HN.

Housing Corporation, 149 Tottenham Court Road, London W1P 0BN.

Small Firms Service, 8-10 Bulstrode Street, London W1. (Tel. 01-487 4342).

Commission for Local Administration in England, 21 Queen Anne's Gate, London SW1H 9BU (Tel. 01-930 3333).

Charity Commission for England and Wales:
Southern Office — 14 Ryder Street, St. James's, London SW1Y 6AH (Tel. 01-214 6000).

Northern Office — Graeme House, Derby Square, Liverpool L2 (Tel. 051-227 3191).

Central Register — St. Alban's House, 57-60 Haymarket, London SW1Y 4QX (Tel. 01-214 6000).

Registrar of Companies, Companies House, Maindy, Cardiff (Tel. 0222-38858).

Registry of Friendly Societies, 17 North Audley Street, London W1Y 2AP (Tel. 01-629 7001).

Inland Revenue Claims Department:
England, Wales & Northern Ireland: Magdalen House, Stanley Precinct, Bootle, Lancs. L69 9BB.
Scotland: Trinity Park House, South Trinity Road, Edinburgh EH5 3SD.

National Co-operative Development Agency, 20 Albert Embankment, London SE1 7TJ.

Who does what in Local Government

COUNTY COUNCILS

Metropolitan County Councils	Non-Metropolitan County Councils	Greater London Council
Consumer protection	Consumer protection	Fire Services
Fire services	Education	◆Land drainage
Highways, traffic and passenger transport	Fire services	Main roads, traffic, passenger transport
◆Land drainage	Highways, traffic and passenger transport co-ordination	◆Museums and arts
Limited housing powers		◆Parking
◆Museums and the arts	◆Land drainage	◆Recreation
Parking	★Library services	Refuse disposal
Police services	Limited housing powers	Some housing powers
◆Recreation	◆Museums and the arts	Strategic planning
Refuse disposal	Parking	
Small holdings	Personal social services	**Inner London**
Strategic planning	Police services	**Education Authority**
◆Town development	◆Recreation	Education
	#Refuse disposal	
	Small holdings	
	Strategic planning	
	◆Town development	

DISTRICT COUNCILS

Metropolitan District Councils

Education
Environmental health
Housing
◆Land drainage
Library services
Local sewers
Minor urban roads
   maintenance
◆Museums and arts
■Off-street parking
Personal social services
◆Recreation
Refuse collection
◆Town development

Non-Metropolitan District Councils

Environmental health
Housing
◆Land drainage
Local planning
Local sewers
Minor urban
   roads maintenance
◆Museums and arts
■Recreation
Refuse collection
Town development

London Borough

Education (outer
   boroughs only)
Environmental health
Housing
◆Land drainage
Libraries
Local sewers
Minor roads
◆Museums and arts
Personal social services
◆Recreation
Refuse collection
◆Town development

Key:
◆Functions shared with other Local Authorities.
★In some parts of Wales these functions are exercised by District Councils.
■These functions are subject to the consent of the County Council.
#These functions are exercised by District Councils in Wales.

13 APPENDICES

SICKLE CELL SOCIETY

CONSTITUTION

1. **NAME**

The name of the association is "Sickle Cell Society" (herein called "the association").

2. **OBJECTS**

The objects of the association are:—

A. The relief of persons suffering from sickle cell anaemia;

B. The provision of facilities for recreation or other leisure time occupation for such persons and for such immediate members of their families having need of such facilities by reason of their youth, age, infirmity or disablement, poverty or social and economic circumstances with the object of improving the conditions of life for such persons.

In furtherance of the above objects but not further or otherwise the association shall have the following powers:—

C. To promote research into sickle cell anaemia and to publish the results of such research.;

D. To collect and diffuse information and advice on sickle cell anaemia to sufferers of the disease and members of the general public by means of forums, lectures, classes, meetings, films and by any other means that the Committee think fit;

E. To assist in the provision of facilities for testing, screening and treating people in connection with sickle cell anaemia;

F. To raise funds required for the achievement of the above objects by any lawful means, provided that the Committee shall not undertake any permanent trading activities in raising funds for the said objects;

G. To employ such persons (not being a member of the commmittee or a Trustee) on such terms as may seen necessary;

H. To enter any arrangements with any government or authority, supreme municipal, local or otherwise, and obtain from such government or authority any rights, privileges and concessions and carry out, exercise and comply with any such arrangements, rights, privileges and concessions;

I. To promote, organise and assist in the organisation and activities of any local group or branch of the association which is formed for the purpose of achieving the above objects or part of them and which functions in accordance with rules and guidelines for the time being made by the association for the conduct of local groups and branches;

J. To do all such other things as are necessary to the attainment of the above objects.

Provided that the association shall not have power to do anything which may cause it to cease to be a charity in law.

196

3. MEMBERSHIP

A. Members
Membership of the association shall be open for any person who supports the objects of the association.

B. Subscription
The amount and date or dates of payment of members' and affiliated organisations' subscriptions shall be set by the Annual General Meeting. The Committee may waive the subscription of any member or affiliated organisation on the grounds of hardship.

C. Cesser of Membership
(i) The membership of any member shall cease on his or her death or on his or her ceasing to reside in the United Kingdom or on his or her membership being terminated in accordance with the next sub-paragraph. (ii) The Committee may terminate the membership of any member whose conduct the Committee consider to be detrimental to the association provided (a) that an attempt has been made by the Committee to draw the matter of complaint to the attention of the member concerned and to resolve any dispute by conciliation and (b) that the member concerned shall have been given at least one week's notice of the meeting at which the question of his or her expulsion is to be discussed together with details of the allegations and an opportunity to be heard by the Committee.

D. Affiliated Organisations
The Committee may allow any organisation to affiliate to the association on such terms as it thinks fit and may terminate the affiliation of any such organisation. Each affiliated organisation shall be entitled to notice of all general meetings of the association and may send an observer to such meetings who may speak but may not vote.

4. MEMBERS MEETINGS

A. Annual General Meeting
The association shall hold an Annual General Meeting at least once in every year in the month of June. The business of the Annual General Meeting shall be: the consideration of the accounts of the association and the Committee's report, the election of members of the Committee, the fixing of subscriptions, the appointment of auditors and any other business of which proper notice shall have been given.

B. Extraordinary General Meeting
An Extraordinary General Meeting shall be convened either by the Committee or on the written requisition of not less than 25% of the members for the time being of the association, such requisition specifying the business proposed to be transacted at the meeting.

C. Notice of General Meetings
Notice of General Meetings shall be given by posting the same to the address of each member shown in the register at least 21 days before the date of the meeting. Such notice shall specify the time and place of the meeting and the business proposed to be transacted at the meeting, including any resolutions proposed to be put to the meeting.

D. Quorum
The quorum at any General Meeting shall be one fifth of the members for the time being of the association. If a quorum is not present within one hour of the time set for the meeting the meeting shall be adjourned to such time and place as shall be determined by the Committee, the Committee giving such notice of such adjournment as it thinks fit.

E. Chairperson
The Chairperson for the time being of the association shall provide at General Meetings and, in his or her absence, the members present may choose one of their number to preside.

F. Procedure at General Meetings
Subject to this constitution the procedure at General Meetings shall be determined by the members in General Meetings shall be determined by the members in General Meeting.

5. COMMITTEE

A. Functions
The affairs of the association shall be managed by a Committee (herein referred to as "the Committee") which may exercise all the powers of the association and do on behalf of the association all such things as are not by this constitution required to be done by the association in General Meeting, subject nevertheless to any resolution of the association in General Meeting. The Committee may delegate any of its powers to a sub-committee or sub-committees and on such terms as it thinks fit.

B. Composition
The Committee shall consist of the following persons who shall be elected at the Annual General Meeting: a Chairperson, a Secretary, a Treasurer and nine other members of the association. Committee members shall hold office from the end of the Annual General Meeting at which they are elected until the end of the next Annual General Meeting and shall be eligible for re-election.

C. Co-options
The Committee may co-opt up to three additional persons, whether members of the association or not. Co-opted members may attend and speak, but may not vote, at Committee meetings.

D. Sub-Committees
A majority of the members of every sub-committee shall be members of the Committee. Subject as aforesaid any sub-committee shall consist of such persons, whether members or not of this association, as the Committee shall determine. Provided that any member of any sub-committee who is not a member of the association may not vote at meetings of the sub-committee. All acts and proceedings of such sub-committees shall be reported back to the Committee as soon as possible.

E. Meetings
The Committee shall meet at least ten times in each year between Annual General Meetings. The quorum at Committee meetings shall be five elected members present at the start of the meeting and no business may be

198

transacted at the meeting of the Committee if less than one third of the elected members are present.

F. Chairperson
The Chairperson for the time being of the association shall preside at Committee meetings and in his or her absence the elected Committee members present shall choose one of their number to preside.

G. Non-Attendance at Committee Meetings
Any member of the Committee who fails to attend three consecutive Committee meetings shall cease to be a member of the Committee unless he or she gives a reason which is, in the opinion of the Committee, satisfactory.

H. Procedure at Committee Meetings
Subject to this Constitution the procedure at Committee meetings shall be determined by the Committee.

6. REGISTER

The Secretary shall keep a register showing the names and addresses of the members of the association and, on being notified in writing of any change, shall alter the register accordingly.

7. NOTICE

Any notice required by the constitution to be given to any person may be given by posting the same in a pre-paid letter to the registered address of that person.

8. TRUSTEES

Up to four trustees may be appointed by the Committee and the property of the association (other than cash) shall be vested in them to be dealt with by them as the Committee shall from time to time decide. The trustees shall be indemnified against loss and expense out of the association's property. They shall hold office until death or resignation or until removed from office by the Committee who may for any reason which may seem sufficient to a majority of them present and voting at a meeting remove any trustees or trustee from office. The Committee may by resolution nominate any person to fill a vacancy in the trustees or to be an additional trustee. For the purpose of giving effect to any such nomination the Chairperson is hereby nominated as the person to appoint new trustees of the association within the meaning of section 36 of the Trustee Act 1925. Any statement of fact in any such deed of appointment shall in favour of a person dealing bona fide and for value with with the association or the Committee be conclusive of the fact so stated.

9. ACCOUNTS

The Treasurer shall cause proper accounts to be kept showing sums of money received and spent by the association, sales and purchases of goods by the association and the assets and liabilities of the association. The accounts shall be audited at least once in every year and presented to the Annual General Meeting of the association.

10. CHANGE OF CONSTITUTION

The provisions of this constitution may be changed by a resolution passed at a General Meeting by a majority of not less than two thirds of those present and voting thereon. But no such change may be made which would have the effect of making the association cease to be a charity in law. Provided that no alteration is made to clause 2, 11 or this clause without previously consulting the Charity Commission.

11. WINDING UP

The association may be wound up by a resolution passed at a General Meeting by a majority of not less than two thirds of those present and voting thereon. Any assets remaining after satisfaction of all debts and liabilities shall not be distributed amongst the members of the association but shall be given or transferred to some other charitable organisation or organisations having similar objects.

FELTHAM COMMUNITY ASSOCIATION CONSTITUTION

1. ## NAME

   The name of the Association shall be the Feltham Community Association (hereinafter called "the Association").

2. ## OBJECTS

   The objects of the Association shall be:-

   a) To promote the benefit of the persons living and/or having permanent employment in Feltham (defined as the electoral wards of Feltham/ Bedfont hereinafter called the "Area of Benefit", without distinction of sex, sexual orientation, race or colour, or of political, religious or other opinions by associating the Local Authorities, voluntary organisations and individuals in a common effort to advance education and provide facilities in the interests of social welfare for recreation and leisure time occupation with the object of improving the conditions of life for the said persons.

   b) To establish or to secure the establishment of a Community Centre (hereinafter called "The Centre") and to maintain and manage, or to co-operate with any local statutory authority in the maintenance and management of such a Centre for activities promoted by the Associated and its Constituent Bodies in furtherance of the above objects.

   The Association shall be non-party in politics and non-sectarian in religion. The Association shall have the power to affiliate to the National Federation of Community Organisations and to other organisations with similar charitable objects.

3. ## ANCILLARY POWERS

   In furtherance of the Association's objects but not further or otherwise, the Association shall have the following powers:-

   a) To build, construct, alter, maintain, pull down, remove or replace and to work, manage and control any buildings works or convenience when the Association may think necessary or convenient for the purpose of the aforesaid.

   b) To receive money on deposit or loan and borrow or raise money in such a manner as the Association shall think fit subject to such consent as required by law.

   c) To do all such lawful things as may be necessary to the attainment of the Association's charitable objects.

4. ## MEMBERSHIP

   Membership of the Association shall be of two kinds:

   a) Individuals who shall be full, junior, associate, temporary members and honorary life members.

   b) Groups which shall be the constituent bodies and sections as hereinafter defined.

201

5. INDIVIDUAL MEMBERSHIP

Individual membership shall be open irrespective of political party, nationality, religious opinion, race or colour, sex or sexual orientation, to -

a) All persons living and/or having permanent employment in the area of benefit aged 18 years or over who shall be called FULL MEMBERS.

b) All persons living and/or having permanent employment in the area of benefit under the age of 18 who shall be called JUNIOR MEMBERS.

Junior Members on or after attaining the age of 16 may be granted upon written application and payment of such additional subscription as the Council may determine, the benefits of full membership. Junior members, other than those granted the rights of full membership, shall not have the right to vote at General Meetings but may elect from among themselves two representatives to the Council, who shall both have the right to vote.

c) Well wishers living anywhere outside the area of benefit who shall be called ASSOCIATE MEMBERS. Associate members shall not have the right to vote at General Meetings but may elect from among themselves one representative to the Council who shall have the right to vote.

d) The manner in which Junior and Associate Members elect their representatives shall be determined by the FCA Council from time to time.

e) The Association may grant temporary membership to individuals and groups visiting the Centre, for a period of 24 hours ending at midnight on the day of the visit. Temporary members will not be entitled to vote at any meeting of the Association. The grant of temporary membership shall be posted on Association Noticeboards at least 48 hours before temporary membership takes effect.

f) The Council may from time to time bestow Honorary Life Membership on individuals for their service to the Association. Honorary Life Members will be entitled to all the benefits of a full member of the Association.

6. GROUP MEMBERSHIP

a) Constituent Bodies shall be the local statutory authorities and such voluntary organisations as operate in the area of benefit and satisfy the FCA Council that they are independent organisations or branches of independent organisations, national or otherwise and who agree to abide by the objects of the Association.

b) Sections shall be such groups as may, with the permission of the Council, be formed within the Association among the individual members for the furtherance of a common activity.

Each constituent body and section (except the youth section) who shall have the right to appoint two in accordance with clause 5 (b), shall have the right to appoint one representative to be a member of the Council and at any time, by giving notice in writing to the Secretary of the Association, to revoke such appointment and to appoint another representative in his/her place. Constituent body representatives shall not have the benefits of full membership of the Association but shall have the right to vote at General Meetings.

7. TERMINATION OF MEMBERSHIP

The FCA Council shall have the right for good and sufficient reasons to terminate the membership of an individual member or of a constituent body or section provided that the individual member or person representing the body or section shall have the right to be heard by the Council before a decision is made.

In the event of the misconduct of an individual member or individual member's guest/s, likely to give rise to the Council's consideration of termination of membership (or in the case of a guest, refuse future entry of the guest), any Honorary Officer of the Association or of the Council, full time Administrators and such other members of the Council as the Council may from time to time determine, shall have the right to suspend membership or bar guests from entry subject to the rights contained in this clause. Such suspension of membership or barring of guests must be placed as an agenda item for discussion at the next Executive Committee or Executive Sub-Committee. The Executive Committee or Executive Sub-Committee shall have the right, for good and sufficient reason to endorse the suspension action on the individual member and/or recommend termination of membership to be considered by the next Council Meeting, provided that the individual member shall have the right to be heard by the Executive Committee or Executive Sub-Committee before a decision is made. The Executive Committee or Executive Sub-Committee shall, in addition, have the right to suspend the individual member's privilege of bringing guests and refuse any future entry of the guests involved in misconduct.

8. SUBSCRIPTIONS

All members and Constituent Bodies shall pay such subscriptions as the Council may from time to time determine.

9. THE COUNCIL

Subject to the limitations set out in Clause 11 hereof, the policy and general management of the affairs of the Association shall be directed by a Council (hereinafter referred to as "The Council") which shall meet not less than three times a year.

The Council shall consist of:-

a) (i) The representatives appointed by the Constituent Bodies and sections in accordance with clause 6 but so that not more than 10 representatives of constituent bodies and 10 representatives of sections may have the right to vote.

(ii) If the number of representatives exceeds the above stated numbers, then those representatives with the right to vote shall be elected by the Annual General Meeting (AGM).

b) Such number of full members to be elected from among and by themselves at the AGM as is of equal to the number of Council members appointed with the right to vote under Clause 9 (a) (ii); and in any case not less than eight.

c) Two representatives of junior members elected in accordance with Clause 5 (b).

d) One representative of Associate members elected in accordance with Clause 5 (c).

e) The Honorary Officers of the Association and of the Council ex-officio in accordance with Clause 10 (a).

f) 2/4 representatives appointed by the Trustees if Trustees shall have been appointed in accordance with Clause 17.

g) Such persons employed by or seconded to the Association as the Council may from time to time determine in accordance with Clause 10 (b).

In addition, the Council may co-opt further members who shall be members of the Association provided that the number of co-opted members shall not exceed one-third of the total number of members of the Council as defined above.

All members of the Council shall retire annually but shall be eligible to be appointed or co-opted again. The Council shall have the power to appoint such committees as it may from time to time decide and may determine their powers and terms of reference.

10. OFFICERS

a) Honorary Officers

The Annual General Meeting shall elect a President, a Treasurer and such other Officers of the Association, such as Honorary Secretary, as it may from time to time determine. The Council shall elect its Chair and such other Officers as it may from time to time determine. The Chair of the Council shall be ex-officio Chair of the Executive Committee.

All Honorary Officers of the Association and of the Council shall be ex-officio members of the Executive and all other Committees.

b) Paid Officers

The Council shall have power to appoint and dismiss a (paid) Secretary and such other employees of the Association as it may from time to time determine.

The Council (and only the Council) may determine which (if any) persons employed by or seconded to the Association shall be members ex-officio of the Council, the Executive and all other committees. Persons employed by or seconded to the Association shall not have voting rights on any subject concerned with pay and conditions of employment.

The Council shall ensure that Contracts of Employment are drawn up and that these conform with relevant employment legislation protecting the interests of both employer and employee.

The Council may appoint an Officer (hereinafter referred to as the "Designated Officer") who shall be responsible for the day to day industrial relations between employer and employee.

11. ANNUAL GENERAL MEETING

Once in each year, in the month of May, the Council shall convene an Annual

General Meeting, which all individual members and representatives of the constituent bodies and sections will be entitled to attend. This will be for the purpose of receiving reports on the year's work, accepting balance sheets, accepting resignations and electing representatives from full members to serve on the Council, electing representatives of constituent bodies and sections with a right to vote to serve on the Council if necessary in accordance with Clause 9 (a) (ii), electing Honorary Officers of the Association from among these members who are entitled to vote, also appointing auditor(s), of making recommendations to the Council and whenever necessary of voting on proposals to amend the Constitution in accordance with Clause 19 hereof.

12. SPECIAL GENERAL MEETING

The Chair of the Council or the Secretary may at any time at their discretion, and shall within twenty-one days of receiving a written request to do so, signed by not less than 30 members having the power to vote and giving reasons for the request, call a Special General Meeting of the Association for the purpose of altering the Constitution in accordance with Clause 19 hereof or of considering any matter which may be referred to them by the Council or for any other purpose.

13 EXECUTIVE COMMITTEE

At its first meeting following the Annual General Meeting in each year, the Council shall appoint an Executive Committee to which it may delegate any or all of its powers as it may from time to time determine.

The Executive Committee in accordance with the wishes of the Council shall consist of members elected by and from the members of the Council and of the Officers of the Association and of the Council hereinbefore provided. The Executive Committee shall have the power to co-opt additional members who shall be members of the Association but need not be members of the Council provided that the number of co-opted members does not exceed one third of the total number of elected and ex officio members. All members of the Executive Committee shall retire annually but shall be eligible to be appointed or co-opted again.

The Executive Committee shall have the power to appoint such sub-committees as it may from time to time decide and may determine their powers and terms of reference provided that all acts and proceedings of such sub-committees shall be reported to the Executive Committee in due course.

14. RULES OF PROCEDURE AT ALL MEETINGS

a) Voting

Subject to the provisions of Clause 19, all questions arising at any meeting shall be decided by a simple majority of those present and entitled to vote thereat. No member shall exercise more than one vote notwithstanding that he or she may have been appointed to represent two or more interests but in case of an equality of votes, the Chair shall have a second or casting vote.

b) Quorum

One third of the members shall form a quorum at meetings of the Council, Executive and all other Committees. A quorum must consist of at least two thirds elected officers. Thirty-five members shall form a quorum at General Meetings of the Association.

c) Minutes

Minute books shall be kept by the Association, the Executive, the Council and all other sub-committees and the appropriate Secretary shall enter therein a record of all proceedings and resolutions.

15. STANDING ORDERS AND RULES FOR THE USE OF THE CENTRE

The Executive Committee shall have power to adopt and issue Standing Orders and Rules for the use of the Centre. Such Standing Orders and Rules shall come into operation immediately providing always that they shall be subject to review by the Council and shall not be inconsistent with the provisions of this Constitution.

16. FINANCE

a) Covenants, Occupation Licence Rents, Gifts, Donations and all monies raised by or on behalf of the Association shall be applied to further the charitable objects of the Association.

b) The Honorary Treasurer shall keep proper accounts of the finances of the Association.

c) The accounts shall be audited at least once a year by a qualified auditor or auditors who shall be appointed at the Annual General Meeting.

d) An audited Statement of Accounts for the last financial year shall be submitted by the Council to the Annual General Meeting.

17. TRUST PROPERTY

The title of all and any real property which may be acquired by or for the purposes of the Association shall be vested in Trustees who shall be appointed by the Council and who shall enter into a Deed of Trust setting forth the purposes and conditions under which they hold the said property in trust for the Association. The number of Trustees shall be not less than 2 nor more than 4.

18. DISSOLUTION

If the Council by a simple majority decides at any time that on the grounds of expense or otherwise it is necessary or advisable to dissolve the Association, it shall call a meeting of all members of the Association who have the power to vote and of the persons of the Area of Benefit of the age of 18 years and upwards of which not less than 21 days notice (stating the terms of the resolution to be proposed thereat) shall be posted in a conspicuous place or places in the area of benefit and advertised in a newspaper circulating in the area of benefit and given in writing to the Charity Commission for England and Wales and the Secretary for the National Federation of Community

Organisations. If such a decision shall be confirmed by a simple majority of those present and voting at such meeting the Council shall have power to dispose of any assets held by or in the name of the Association. Any assets remaining after the satisfaction of any proper debts and liabilities shall not be distributed among the members of the Association but shall be applied towards charitable purposes for the benefit of the persons of the area of benefit as the Council may decide and as may be approved by the Charity Commissioners for England and Wales.

19. ALTE.LATIONS TO THE CONSTITUTION

Any proposal to alter this constitution must be delivered in writing to the Secretary of the Association not less than 28 days before the date of the meeting at which it is first to be considered. Any alteration will require the consideration of the Council and the approval of a two-thirds majority of individual members and representatives of Constituent Bodies and sections of the Association present and voting at a General Meeting. Notice of such a meeting must be given in accordance with normal procedures but not less than 14 days prior to the meeting in question and giving the wording of the proposed alteration. No alteration to Clause 2 shall be made without the prior consent in writing of the Charity Commissioners for England and Wales. No alteration shall be made which would cause the Association to cease to be a charity at law.

If Trustees have been appointed in accordance with Clause 17 hereof, an alteration shall not be made without the knowledge and consent of the Trustees, but such consent shall not be unreasonably withheld by them.

This Constitution was adopted as the amended Constitution of the Feltham Community Association at a meeting of members duly convened at the Feltham Community Centre on:-

N.B.

The National Federation of Community Organisations agreed in 1983 a simplified version of this constitution with the Charity Commissioners.

It has a more extensive list of powers and a single governing committee, rather than a Council and Executive Committee.

Copies can be obtained from NFCO, price 30p each plus 20p p & p.